W9-ARY-936

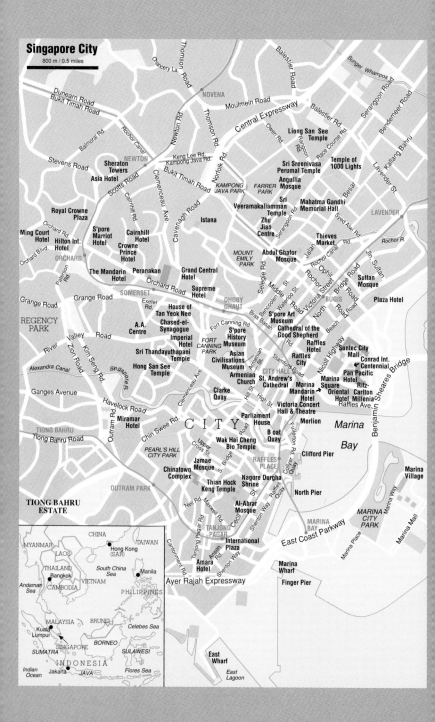

Singapore City

800 m / 0.5 miles

Thomson Road
Orancery La.
Chancery La.
Balestier Road
Sungei Whampoa
Dunearn Road
Bukit Timah Road
NOVENA
Moulmein Road
Balestier Rd.
Central Expressway
Owen Rd.
Liong San See Temple
Serangoon Road
Bendemeer Road
Stevens Road
Balmoral Rd.
Rochor Canal
Newton Rd.
NEWTON
Keng Lee Rd.
Kampong Java Rd.
Norfolk Rd.
Rangoon Rd.
Race Course Rd.
Kallang Bahru
Sheraton Towers
Asia Hotel
Scotts Road
Bukit Timah Road
KAMPONG JAVA PARK
FARRER PARK
Sri Sreenivasa Perumal Temple
Angullia Mosque
Temple of 1000 Lights
Besar
Lavender St.
LAVENDER
Royal Crowne Plaza
Cairnhill Rd.
Clemenceau Ave.
Cavenagh Road
Istana
Sri Veeramakaliamman Temple
Serangoon Rd.
Mahatma Gandhi Memorial Hall
Syed Alwi Rd.
Ming Court Hotel
Hilton Int. Hotel
S'pore Marriot Hotel
Cairnhill Hotel
Crowne Prince Hotel
Zhu Jiao Centre
Thieves Market
Jalan Besar
Rochor R.
Jln. Sultan
ORCHARD
Orchard Rd.
Orchard Blvd.
Paterson Rd.
The Mandarin Hotel
Peranakan
Grand Central Hotel
MOUNT EMILY PARK
Abdul Ghafor Mosque
Selegie Rd.
Middle Rd.
Rochor Ophir
Bridge Road
Sultan Mosque
Plaza Hotel
Grange Road
SOMERSET
Orchard Road
Supreme Hotel
DHOBY GHAUT
Bras Basah Rd.
Bencoolen St.
Waterloo St.
Victoria St.
North Bridge Road
Beach Road
BUGIS
REGENCY PARK
Grange Road
Exeter Rd.
House of Tan Yeok Nee
Fort Canning Rd.
S'pore Art Museum
S'pore Museum
Cathedral of the Good Shepherd
Raffles Hotel
Suntec City Mall
River Valley Road
A.A. Centre
Chased-el-Synagogue
Imperial Hotel
FORT CANNING PARK
S'pore History Museum
Armenian St.
Stamford Road
Raffles City
Nicoll Highway
Conrad Int. Centennial
Kim Seng Rd.
Zion Road
Singapore R.
Sri Thandayuthapani Temple
Hong San See Temple
Asian Civilisations Museum
Armenian Church
St. Andrew's Cathedral
CITY HALL
Marina Mandarin Hotel
Marina Square
Pan Pacific Hotel
Ritz-Carlton Hotel
Oriental Hotel
Millenia
Benjamin Sheares Bridge
Alexandra Canal
Ganges Avenue
Havelock Road
Clemenceau Ave.
Clarke Quay
Hill St.
High St.
Victoria Concert Hall & Theatre
Raffles Ave.
TIONG BAHRU
Tiong Bahru Road
Miramar Hotel
Outram Rd.
Chin Swee Rd.
CITY
Parliament House
B oat Quay
Merlion
Fullerton Rd.
Marina Bay
PEARL'S HILL CITY PARK
Upper Cross St.
Wak Hai Cheng Bio Temple
South Bridge Rd.
RAFFLES PLACE
Clifford Pier
Collyer Quay
Marina Village
OUTRAM PARK
Chinatown Complex
Jamae Mosque
Thian Hock Keng Temple
Nagore Durgha Shrine
North Pier
Raffles Quay
TIONG BAHRU ESTATE
Neil Rd.
Maxwell Rd.
Al-Abrar Mosque
Cecil St.
Shenton Way
MARINA BAY
East Coast Parkway
MARINA CITY PARK
Marina Way
Marina Mall
Cantonment Rd.
Tanjong Pagar Rd.
Anson Rd.
TANJONG PAGAR
International Plaza
Marina Place
Amara Hotel
Shenton Way
Ayer Rajah Expressway
Marina Wharf
Finger Pier

CHINA
MYANMAR
LAOS
TAIWAN
THAILAND
Bangkok
VIETNAM
Hong Kong (SAR)
South China Sea
Manila
Andaman Sea
CAMBODIA
PHILIPPINES
Celebes Sea
MALAYSIA
BRUNEI
Kuala Lumpur
BORNEO
SULAWESI
SUMATRA
SINGAPORE
INDONESIA
Indian Ocean
Jakarta
JAVA
Flores Sea

East Wharf
East Lagoon

SINGAPORE

APA PUBLICATIONS

Part of the Langenscheidt Publishing Group

Welcome!

Singapore is renowned, not only as a melting pot of Asian culture and a great city for a shopping spree, but also as one of the culinary centres of Asia. Modernity and tradition go hand in hand in this city-state, so don't be too alarmed if you come across a jumble of red-tiled roofs with occupants who practise ancestral worship beside towering skyscrapers and luxury hotels. Annual festivals and religious celebrations add colour and excitement to this thriving nation.

All the must-see sights are included: the colonial heart of the city, the business district, downtown Orchard Road, the ethnic enclaves of the Chinese, Malays and Indians, plus lesser-known and quieter hideaways like Sungei Buloh Nature Park and Changi. For those who find themselves hemmed in by city life, there are excursions further afield – to idyllic Bintan island in Indonesia, a Malaysian city across the border, and a romantic rail journey on the E & O Express to Bangkok.

 Marianne Rankin, Insight's Singapore correspondent, first arrived in the city with her husband in 1985 as expatriates. She found herself with a new place to explore and a whole new life ahead of her. Even though she has been in Singapore for over a decade, Rankin is still discovering new and fascinating nooks behind the glittering facades of Singapore's soaring hotels and shopping centres. She has suggested itineraries which reflect both the old and new and has, of course, included her favourite eating haunts and bargain shops.

CONTENTS

Pages 2/3:
The Singapore skyline
from the lofty perch of
the Westin Stamford

Excursions

Eating Out & Shopping

Calendar of Events

Practical Information

Pages 8/9:
Religion plays a central
role in the lives of most
Singapore youths

Maps

HISTORY & CULTURE

Singapore has grown from an outpost on the old East-West trade route to the busiest port in the world today, having a reputation as a stable and efficient base for expansion in the Southeast Asian region. It is tempting to view Singapore as the creation of two men – Sir Stamford Raffles, who founded the city in 1819, and Mr Lee Kuan Yew, who as Prime Minister led it to prosperity after independence in 1965. Although a convenient simplification, the two names and dates are without doubt the most significant in the history of Singapore.

The Founding of Singapore

Not much is known about Singapore's distant past. Mere mentions in ancient Chinese texts precede the legendary changing of its name from Temasek, or 'Sea Town', recorded in the *Malay Annals*.

The story goes that the Srivijayan ruler Sang Nila Utama, who had taken the title Sri Tri Buana, was on his way to explore the inviting sands of Temasek when a storm almost overturned his ship. Throwing even his crown into the sea to lighten the load, he finally landed safely on the island. There, he caught sight of a strange creature with a red body, black head and white breast, which was

Singapore River in its early days

incorrectly identified as a lion. Thus, the island acquired the name 'Lion City' or in Sanskrit – Singapura.

Sri Tri Buana's settlement prospered due to its position on the trade route between China, Persia and Arabia. This aroused envy in his neighbours, and led to many invasion attempts, with Singapura eventually becoming part of the Javanese Majapahit Empire. After that, little is known until the early 19th century, by which time it was under the rule of the Sultan of Johor through his representative on the island, the Temenggong.

Modern Singapore began with the landing of Sir Stamford Raffles, then Lieutenant-Governor of Bencoolen, on 28 January 1819. His task was to set up a trading post for the East India Company to compete with Dutch dominance in the region. This he achieved by means of a treaty with Sultan Hussein of Johor and the Temenggong, signed on 6 February 1819.

Shophouses along Boat Quay

Raffles began to organise the settlement and – despite frequent absences when Resident Colonel Farquhar was in charge – he was ultimately responsible for the layout of the city. He determined the location of the government sector, the European town, and areas for the Bugis, Arab, Chulia and Malay communities. Chinatown was organised so that the Chinese of different classes and from different provinces lived in their own sections within the area to the southwest of the Singapore River. The construction of masonry houses with tiled roofs was also prescribed by Raffles, as are the 'five-foot way' or covered pavement.

Immigration, mainly of Chinese from Malacca, increased the population to 5,000 by June 1819. Trade flourished and the settlement grew in prosperity although slave trading also thrived, as did opium smoking and prostitution.

The British took full possession of the island in 1824 under Raffles' leadership. Raffles was succeeded by John Crawford. The island was by then home to 11,000 people, mostly Malays, and with a large number of Chinese and Bugis, and fewer Indians, Europeans, Armenians and Arabs.

In 1826, Singapore became part of the Straits Settlements. By 1832, it was the centre of government and on 1 April 1867, the Straits Settlements became a Crown Colony. Singapore's status was elevated when it became an important port and coaling station on the route through the Suez Canal from Europe to the Far East. By this time, the rubber industry in Malaya was taking off as a result of botanist Henry Ridley's experiments with the crop. Rubber soon become the main commodity of trade and export was handled through

Singapore. The economy boomed and the future looked secure.

The Japanese conquest on 15 February 1942 shattered the lives of colonials and locals alike, and nothing was ever the same again. For 3ˇ years, Singapore, renamed Syonan-to (Light of the South), was under Japanese rule, with the former colonial masters incarcerated. After the Japanese surrender in 1945, the British returned and, for several years, attempted to retain their former hold on the colony. But times and attitudes had changed, and the British were never able to regain their former prestige after the humiliation of their quick defeat in 1942.

Independence was in the air, and after various attempts at compromise by the British against a background of insurrection led by the Communist Party of Malaya, Singapore finally attained self government on 5 June 1959. Lee Kuan Yew was sworn in as Prime Minister, having led his People's Action Party (PAP) to victory in the first General Election.

Merger with Malaya in a Federation of Malaysia with Sabah and Sarawak took place on 16 September 1963, to the displeasure of neighbouring Indonesia, which then began three years of armed confrontation with the Federation. Racial tensions and political differences soon led to a split with Kuala Lumpur, and on 9 August 1965, Singapore withdrew from the Federation and became an independent nation.

Lee Kuan Yew and his team then began the process of nation building in earnest, coping with immediate basic problems of housing, unemployment and political unrest. During the late 1960s and in the 1970s the PAP was able to turn their attention to building up the infrastructure, attracting foreign investment and moving Singapore into higher skilled industries, away from the cheap labour market towards developed nation status.

Political stability has been maintained through the 1980s and

Singapore's future lies in the hands of its young people

with an eye to the future, the Old Guard leaders have made way for new blood. On 28 November 1990, after 31 years as Prime Minister, Lee Kuan Yew handed over the reins of power to his chosen successor Goh Chok Tong and his team of second generation leaders. It was a smooth transition, the culmination of his policy of preparing Singapore for life without the 'father of the nation'. Elections held in 1991 retained the PAP in power, under Goh Chok Tong, with a total of four opposition members. Lee Kuan Yew 're-tired' but continues in the political sphere as Senior Minister, dispensing advice from time to time. At Singapore's first presidential elections held in August 1993, Ong Teng Cheong, the former Deputy Prime Minister, became the nation's first elected president. In the 1997 general elections, the PAP under Prime Minister Goh won 65 percent of the vote and 81 out of 83 seats in parliament.

Since 1990, Goh has moved towards a 'more open, people-oriented' consensus style of government, in part to appease growing dissatisfaction among the educated elite over its authoritarian style. Although some changes have taken place – a move towards a freer press and the screening of 'R' rated movies depicting sex and violence – many see these as superficial moves towards liberalisation.

As Singapore rises to the challenges of the new millennium, the need to keep reinventing itself to stay on top of the pack was made evident by the Asian economic crisis which hit its shores in 1998.

Sparked by the currency devaluation in Thailand in mid-1997, which quickly spread to neighbouring countries like Indonesia, Malaysia and the Philippines, even rock-solid Singapore – with its world's fourth-largest foreign reserves of US$44.15 billion and a 50 percent domestic savings rate – began to feel the impact. In the face of a recession in 1998 and a flat growth in 1999, Singapore is taking steps to ensure that it remains competitive by cutting business costs and stimulating the economy with further infrastructure development plans.

Culture

The pattern of the island and the rhythm of the year spring from the inherent cultural diversity of Singapore. The immigrant peoples have given the place a mélange of Malay, Chinese, Indian and European influences, all of which intermingle and are still evident behind the streamlined facade of the modern city.

Although citizens of all races tend to think of themselves as Singaporean today, and live next to each other throughout the island, the areas designated for the different races by Sir Stamford Raffles still remain, each retaining its unique atmosphere.

As you walk around the streets of Chinatown, or along Arab Street in the Muslim part of the city, or down Serangoon Road in Little India, you can appreciate the unique cultural background of each neighbourhood. All over the city are signs of the British colonial influence – in the Neo-Classical buildings designed by George Coleman and enclaves of gracious black and white houses.

Each racial group has its own religion and all year round there are colourful festivals of special significance for different races enjoyed by all. Decorations go up and come down with remarkable speed. Some places have even been clever enough to use the same decorations for different festivals.

People

The original inhabitants of Singapore were Malay fishermen, and Malay is still the national language, although some say this is mere superficial deference to the indigenous Malays in a largely Chinese-dominated society. Today, Malays make up 14 percent of the 3 million population. Although few are able to maintain their traditional *kampong* (village) life here, as they had to move into highrise flats, they have not changed their priorities. Malays are bound by the Islamic code. For them, family life is more important than material

Modern Chinese

wealth and the chase for worldly gains always tempered with spiritual development. Today, their once laid-back view of life is changing as the pressure mounts on them to keep pace with the commercial world.

That is where the Chinese thrive, from the earliest days of river trade to today's computerised stock market. They account for over 78 percent of the population, and are at the centre of the commercial and political spheres. Although stemming from regions all over China, each with its own culture and dialect, many Singaporean Chinese have lost touch with mainland Chinese traditions. Dialects remain the *lingua franca* of the elderly, but all are now encouraged to speak Mandarin, the preferred second language for Chinese children and youth in schools. Although modern, the Chinese nevertheless prefer to keep on the right side of the gods of fortune, however nebulous they may be. Many are still deeply influenced by age-old traditions and beliefs. Spanking new offices are built and furnished according to ancient *feng shui* (geomancy) principles – this led to the doors of the Grand Hyatt in Scotts Road being realigned at 32 degrees in 1981.

Indians, many originally convicts and indentured labourers from South India, now make up 7 percent of Singaporeans, and are well represented in politics and the law, as well as in journalism and commerce. Most are Hindus and they too carefully preserve their ancient customs and festivals.

Straits-born Chinese, or Peranakans, were the product of inter-marriages between Chinese and Malays. These *baba*s and *nonya*s (men and women) had their own culture and language, but all that remains now is their decorative architecture, colourful ceramics and delicious Peranakan cuisine. Periodically, Peranakan plays are staged to help revive the culture.

Completing the mix of cultures is an expatriate community from all over the world, many staying only for a couple of years, but others settling and making their home here.

Modern Singaporeans of different cultures mix and intermarry more than their predecessors did, with an eye to the western world. However, they still maintain the Asian tradition of respect for their elders and the belief in upholding family ties. On the whole, Singaporeans of today are a hardworking and industrious people, proud of what their small island nation has achieved in its short life.

Religions

Religious tolerance is essential in Singapore, where adherents to the main faiths of the world live and worship cheek by jowl. Religions often cross racial boundaries and some even merge in unusual ways in this cosmopolitan island.

In Chinese temples, Taoism, Confucianism, Buddhism and ancestral worship blend into an eclectic mix. In the early days, the Chinese would erect places of worship on arrival to thank the gods for their safe journey. These later became established temples.

Followers of *Tao*, the Way, adhere to the teachings of the ancient Chinese sage Lao Tzu. They are concerned with the principles of astrology, and the balance of *Yin* and *Yang*, which are the opposite forces of heaven and earth, male and female. Here too is the origin of *feng shui* – literally translated as wind and water – according to

A Chinese wayang (opera) mural

which buildings are located, constructed and furnished. Ancestral worship is common, and the spirits of the dead, like the gods themselves, are appeased with offerings. One of the most popular deities is Kuan Yin, the Goddess of Mercy.

Most Buddhists are of the Mahayana school, although the Theravada school is also represented. But here the faith is linked with Taoism and the practical tenets of Confucianism.

Malays are Muslims, as are some Indians and more rarely so, Chinese. Islam has a fundamental influence in the lives of those who follow Mohammed, the Prophet of Allah, involving prayer five times a day, eating only *halal* food which has been specially prepared in accordance with Islamic law, fasting during Ramadan and going to Mecca on the *Haj* (pilgrimage).

With the arrival of Indian immigrants came Hinduism. The early temples with their intricate figurines of gods are still the focal point of the Hindu rituals and festivals held throughout the year.

Christian churches of all persuasions are to be found in Singapore after Raffles paved the way for the arrival of missionaries. Today, there is a sizeable number of Christians on the island.

Minority faiths are not forgotten: there are two synagogues for the Jews and Sikhs while Zoroastrians and Jains are also represented.

Young Singaporeans tend to take what makes sense from the older generation and blend that with a more pragmatic world outlook. Many Chinese and Indians have become Christians, but the Malays, in general, remain true to Islam.

Many of Singapore's most interesting buildings are religious, whether old temples or modern churches and mosques, and an understanding of the various religions contributes to their appreciation.

Etiquette

What to visitors is a curiosity, to the believer is a matter of deep significance. If you remember that and act accordingly, you'll have no problems with etiquette in the temples of Singapore. Where strict rules apply, there are clear signs to advise you.

Chinese temples are relaxed or slightly chaotic. People pray, bowing with incense sticks clasped between their palms, buy and sell anything from 'hell money', incense and fresh flowers to paper umbrellas, and sit down to eat, all in and around the courtyard. Do remember to ask permission before taking photographs, particularly of elderly people.

In Hindu temples, devotees walk around freely and ceremonies are performed at certain times, often heralded with loud music. Shoes must be removed before entering.

Ladies must be modestly dressed to enter a mosque, and may only enter certain areas. Again, shoes must be removed.

If you enter a Singaporean home, be prepared to take your shoes off and relax and enjoy yourself. Do, however, remember that Asians are more reticent than Westerners in discussing personal matters, and less inclined to public displays of affection.

Historical Highlights

1819: Sir Stamford Raffles sets up a trading post for the British East India Company with the agreement of the Sultan of Johor and the Temenggong, his representative on the island.

1824: The Sultan cedes Singapore in perpetuity to the British.

1826: Singapore, with Malacca and Penang, becomes part of the Straits Settlements, under the control of British India.

1867: The Colonial Office in London takes over control of Singapore.

1942: The Japanese, led by General Tomoyuki Yamashita, invade and occupy Singapore.

1945: The Japanese surrender and the Allied Forces return.

1946: Singapore becomes a Crown Colony.

1955: The Rendel Constitution granted by the British leads to elections and David Marshall becomes Chief Minister.

1956: Lim Yew Hock takes over as Chief Minister.

1958: A Constitutional Agreement for independence for Singapore is signed in London.

1959: The first General Election for a fully elected Legislative Assembly results in Lee Kuan Yew becoming Prime Minister as leader of the victorious People's Action Party (PAP).

1963: Singapore becomes part of the Federation of Malaysia.

1965: Singapore, forced out of the Federation of Malaysia, becomes an independent sovereign nation.

1967: Singapore issues its own currency.

1968: In the general election, the PAP wins all 58 seats.

1981: In a by-election, Mr J B Jeyaratnam of the Workers' Party wins the first seat to be held by an opposition member.

1987: The US$5 billion state-of-the-art Mass Rapid Transit (MRT) light railway system opens.

1988: Under a revised constitution the PAP wins 80 seats in a general election, with the Singapore Democratic Party winning one seat, and two members of the Workers' Party declared non-constituency MPs.

1990: Prime Minister Lee Kuan Yew hands leadership of PAP over to Goh Chok Tong, who forms the new government.

1991: The ruling PAP wins the election again, but this time losing four seats to the opposition.

1993: Ong Teng Cheong is elected as President in Singapore's first presidential election.

1997: PAP under Prime Minister Goh wins all but two parliamentary seats in general election.

1998: Work begins on the north-eastern MRT extension. Second Link, the new causeway to Malaysia opens at Tuas. The economy contracts in the last two quarters as the Asian financial crisis hits Singapore.

1999: Proposed cuts on taxes and the Central Provident Fund (CPF) to remain competitive in light of the worsening recession.

Johor Baharu

Royal Mausoleum
Abu Bakar Mosque
Zoo
Istana Besar
Istana Tengku Mahkota

Selat Johor

MALAYSIA

Putri Narrows
Kelongs

P. BULOH

Kranji Dam

Ng Kay Boon Est.

Woodlands New Town

N15
ADMIRALTY

N16 WOODLANDS

N17 MARSILING

SINGAPORE

Tebing Runtoh

Tg Gedong

Sarimbun Reservoir

Kranji Industrial Estate

N18 KRANJI

Kranji War Memorial

Tg Murai

Lim Chu Kang

Thong Hoe Estate

S. Kangkar

Kranji Res.

Sungai Kadut Industrial Estate

Mandai Road

MANDAI ORCHID GARDENS

Seletar

Murai Res.

Amo Keng

S. Peng Siang

S. Tengah

Woodlands Rd.

Bukit Timah Expressway

SINGAPORE ZOOLOGICAL GARDENS

Seletar Res.

Kankar Pendas

Kg. Pendas

Tg Sopek

Alik Hong and Alik Chiang Estate

Kranji Expressway

N20 YEW TEE

Choa Chu Kang New Town

NATUR RESER

Tg Chengting

Poyan Reservoir

Lam San

Kg Tengah

N21 CHOA CHU KANG

Bukit Panjang New Town

Bukit Panjang

BUKIT PANJA

Tg Pasir Laba

RESTRICTED ZONE

Choa Chu Kang

Bulim

Jalan Bahar

KIAN HONG ESTATE

Hong Kah

N22-BUKIT GOMBAK

Upper Bukit Timah Rd.

Upper Peirce R

Second Link

Tengeh Reservoir

Bukit Batok Rd

Bukit Batok New Town

BUKIT TIMAH NATURE RES.

NATUR RESERV.

Selat Johor

Tuas Checkpoint Complex

Pan-Island Expwy

Upper Jurong Rd

Jurong

W11 LAKESIDE

Jurong West New Town

W10 CHINESE GARDEN

N23 BUKIT BATOK

Pan-Island Expressway

Bukit Timah

RAFFLES PARK

Bukit Turf Club

Dunearn Rd.

S'pore Discovery Centre

W12 BOON LAY

International Rd.

Jurong Lake

Jurong Town

JURONG PARK

Jurong East New Town

W9 JURONG EAST

Singapore Science Centre

Jurong Town Hall

Bukit Timah Road

Jurong Ind.Estate

Tuas Road

Jurong Reptile Park

Jurong Bird Park

West Coast Rd.

Clementi New Town

QUEEN ASTRI. PARK

WOOLLE

Jalan Buroh

Pandan Res.

W1

BOONA VISTA

W6 COMM

Jurong Central Fish Market

W8 CLEMENTI

West Coast Highway

Nat.University of Singapore

Pasir Panjang

W4

P. DAMAR LAUT

Selat Jurong

P. MERLIMAU

P. M. LAUT

WEST POINT GARDEN

W5 QUEENSTOWN

Queensway

Ayer Rajah Expressw

P. PESEK

Kent Ridge

T Blar

P. PESEK KECHIL

Selat Pesek

P. SERAYA

P. RETAN LAUT

Pasir Panjang Rd.

P. AYER CHAWAN

Selat Ayer Merbau

Tg Pangkong

Selat Sakra

Tg Butun

LABRADOR PARK

P. SAKRA

P. AYER MERBAU

Selat Pandan

P. BUKUM

P. BUSING

Tg Da

P. ULAR

P. HANTU

P. BUKUM KECHIL

Tg Romos

P. SEBARO

Selat Salu

RESTRICTED ZONE

P. SUDONG

P. SEMAKAU

P. JONG

Singapore

3.6 km / 2 miles

Day Itineraries

Here are two full-day itineraries which introduce Singapore, both past and present. On the first day, examine the heart of the city with glimpses into its colonial past. On the second day, stroll through the ethnic enclaves of the Chinese, Malays and Indians, the three main communities of Singapore.

There are probably too many places covered in these itineraries and you might not feel like doing everything suggested; so choose whatever sounds interesting. Remember, these itineraries are just guidelines; feel free to wander from the straight and narrow and explore any odd nooks and crannies on the way. As it's hot and

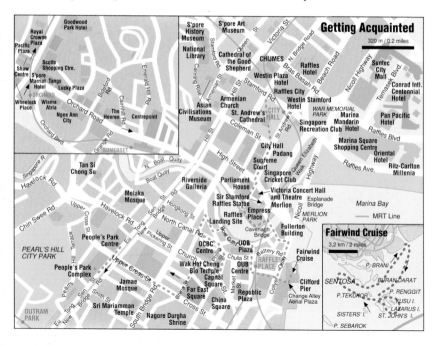

humid here all year round, take taxis for longer trips and save your energy for walking around the more interesting areas. When it gets too hot, just sidetrack into a temple or better still, an air-conditioned department store to cool off.

Remember to drink plenty of water to counteract dehydration, and wear comfortable shoes and clothes made of natural fibre. When it rains in Singapore, it pours buckets, especially in the wet season from November to February, so it's a good idea to take an umbrella with you. Local women preserve their delicate skin by using umbrellas as parasols so you may want to follow suit.

If you're thinking of visiting a mosque, don't forget that, strictly speaking, women should cover their knees and arms before they enter an Islamic place of worship, and keep to the designated areas. Chinese and Indian temples have no such restrictions.

Getting Acquainted

An early morning start visiting St Andrew's Cathedral and the colonial heart of the city; Singapore River, the Central Business District (CBD) and Collyer Quay. Then, a 10.30am harbour cruise on a Chinese-style vessel. A riverside lunch followed by a stroll through Chinatown, perhaps shopping in People's Park before going to Orchard Road for tea and more shopping. Flop out in Peranakan Place for the evening.

Take the Mass Rapid Transit (MRT) to **City Hall** station and the exit for **St Andrew's Cathedral**. Then, walk through the peaceful churchyard into the cool interior of this lovely building. It was built by Indian convicts using a plaster consisting of an extraordinary mixture of egg white, shell, lime, sugar, coconut husk and water known as Madras *chunam*.

Set in peaceful grounds, the present cathedral is the third place of worship to be built on this site. The first, in Palladian style, was designed by George Dromgold Coleman, the Irish ar-

St Andrew's Cathedral and the Westin Stamford

chitect who became Superin-
tendent of Public Works and,
during the years 1828–41, was
responsible for the design of
many of Singapore's loveliest
buildings, including Parliament
House, the Armenian Church
and some of the elegant godowns
or warehouses along the Singapore River.

His church was later altered by James Turnbull Thomson, who
added a tower and steeple, but this was demolished in 1855 after
being struck by lightning twice. The early English-Gothic style
cathedral which now stands was designed by Lieutenant-Colonel
Ronald MacPherson and consecrated in 1862.

A small leaflet detailing the history and brief notes on the
different parts of the cathedral can be found near the side entrance.

Leave the cathedral on the diagonal path leading southwards towards a green expanse known as the **Padang** (Malay for 'field').
This area, formerly known as the Esplanade, has always been at the
centre of life in Singapore. You may see prints of paintings by John
Turnbull Thomson of Coleman's buildings, among them the early
St Andrew's Cathedral, the Armenian Church, and some spacious
bungalows which form the background to the colonial scene at the
Padang's 'Scandal Point'. This end of the field was no doubt thus
named because it was the venue for
evening outings to enjoy the
slightly cooler air; a time and place
to exchange the latest gossip.

With the **Singapore Cricket Club**
(SCC) at the end on the right, the
Singapore Recreation Club (SRC)
on the left, the Padang has had an
interesting past.

The SRC was built on the site of
the *attap* (palm frond) dwelling of
Major Farquhar, the first Resident
and assistant to Raffles. Originally
a club for Eurasians, the SRC was
torn down in 1994 to make way
for a modern building, which was
completed in late 1996. The SCC,
which thankfully still retains its
lovely Victorian-style facade, used
to be exclusively for Europeans.
Nowadays, membership is open to
all at both ends of this green, where
all kinds of activities from cricket
and rugby matches to National
Day celebrations take place.

Supreme Court (left) and City Hall

The Merlion

In 1942, on the day following the Japanese Occupation, European civilians were herded onto the Padang before being marched more than 22km (14 miles) to Changi, where they were imprisoned. Lord Louis Mountbatten accepted the Japanese surrender on the steps of **City Hall**, situated right of the Padang, on 12 September 1945. It was here too that Lee Kuan Yew declared Singapore's independence from Britain in 1959.

Next door to the City Hall is the green-domed **Supreme Court**. Buildings seem to have been erected and pulled down in rapid succession in Singapore since the very early days. The original house by Coleman on this site was remodelled and eventually demolished to enable the Hotel de l'Europe to be built. This was later demolished in 1900 and the Grand Hotel de l'Europe was constructed. This in turn made way for the present Supreme Court building in 1936.

Cross High Street and you'll come to a bronze elephant statue, a gift from the King of Siam, which stands in the gardens of the **Parliament House**. The latter, apart from an extension along the river bank, has survived as Coleman designed it, despite many changes of function, from private house to government offices and courts.

Sir Stamford Raffles

Walk down Parliament Lane, past the splendid **Empress Place Building**, a former government office building. It was converted in the late 80s into a museum which hosted Chinese art and history exhibits. Recently, it was taken over by the National Heritage Board and will re-open in the near future to feature exhibits from other Asian civilisations. Ahead is a statue of Sir Stamford Raffles, on the site of his first landing on the island of Singapore on 28 January 1819.

Turn left along the **Singapore River**. This was once the hub of trade, crammed with bumboats, often with eyes painted on the front, plying between the ships in the harbour and the godowns upriver. Now the water is calm and near empty after a massive clean-up by the government which relocated the boats and filtered the waters. Look across at the fascinating contrast of beautifully restored shophouses towered over by the gleaming high-rise buildings of the **Central Business District (CBD)**.

Just outside Empress Place Building is something which looks rather like Singapore's answer to I M Pei's Louvre pyramid. It is in fact a time capsule sealed in 1990 with items commemorating Singapore's 25 years of independence, to be opened on its 50th anniversary in 2015. Behind Empress Place Building, crowned by a distinctive clock tower, is the lovely white building of the **Victoria**

Memorial Hall and Theatre. In front of this building stands the original sculpture of Raffles by Thomas Woolner, the copy of which you saw by the river. The Singapore Symphony Orchestra gives regular concerts here; check the programme at the booking office within.

And now, for that morning cruise along Singapore's historic waterfront and outlying islands. Make your way over the river by crossing the oldest bridge spanning the river. You won't have to worry about the traffic as **Cavenagh Bridge** is strictly for pedestrians only. You will find yourself in the CBD, amid the bustle of the commercial world. At the main road of **Collyer Quay**, turn right and continue down the road till you

Victoria Memorial Hall and Theatre

Cavenagh Bridge

come to an overhead bridge. Cross over to **Clifford Pier**.

The cruise sets off at 10.30am, so you won't have time to browse around the shops at **Change Alley Aerial Plaza**. You may wish to come back later though as there's everything from electronics to embroidery here.

Down the escalator you will find yourself in a large hall, and right at the end are the offices of two cruise companies. The East Wind company (tel: 533-3422) operates the **Fairwind** harbour cruises on Chinese-style junk boats. The cruise ticket entitles you to refreshments on the boat. Clamber aboard the quaint vessel and look back at Singapore's Wall Street as you drift away past the statue of the **Merlion**, a half-fish, half-lion mythological creature that is a symbol of Singapore.

The **Fullerton Building** is all that remains of the old waterfront, where merchants used to watch their ships as goods were taken ashore by *tongkangs* or lighters, and bumboats. Little boys used to dive into the harbour waters for coins thrown down from the ships, until shark attacks eventually ended their frolics.

So much has changed here. Reclaimed land, traversed by the East Coast Parkway has formed **Marina Bay**. Ships now berth further west where great yellow cranes hoist the huge boxes at the computerised **Tanjong Pagar Container Port** and at four other terminals around the island. The godowns upriver are decaying slowly, although one has been converted into the **Zouk** entertainment complex. The bumboats rocking gently in the water now usually work over in Pasir Panjang or are used to ferry tourists on river tours.

The boat sails out under the **Benjamin Sheares Bridge** to the

Clifford Pier Jetty

Eastern Anchorage where as many as 300 ships from all over the world may be seen, a glimpse of what makes Singapore the world's busiest port. The cruise takes about 2½ hours, so relax and listen to the interesting commentary as you take in the sights. Sun lovers will enjoy the upper deck, while those tired of the heat can watch the scene in air-conditioned comfort below. You'll pass the Container Port, Sentosa Island and the southern islands of St John's, Sisters', Lazarus, Renggit and Kusu, where the vessel will make a 20-minute stop for you to tour the island. Don't miss the **Tua Pek Kong Temple**, where devotees flock to every year for their annual pilgrimage.

On your return, cross over Change Alley Aerial Plaza again, but instead of taking the escalator down to street level, go through the central glass doors on the other side and follow the signs to **Raffles Place**. Formerly known as Commercial Square, this was the hub of colonial life. Here, banks once rubbed shoulders with Robinson's and John Little department stores (where the ladies would meet for morning coffee). Both stores still exist but are now found in Orchard Road. Raffles Place has totally changed today. It is now a pedestrian precinct enveloped by great highrise commercial buildings. The tallest of these skyscrapers is the triumvirate formed by the soaring, acute-angled **OUB Centre** and the equally impressive and newer **UOB Plaza** – both designed by well-known Japanese architect Kenzo Tange – and the most recent addition, the striking blue-facade **Republic Plaza** just across at Market Street. All three are 280-m (920-ft) tall, the maximum height allowed by the local civil aviation authorities.

Proceed for lunch at **Boat Quay**, a lively and popular after-dark venue for young Singaporeans bent on partying all night long. Make your way across Battery Road, straight towards the river,

Raffles Place

turning left along Boat Quay. This was once a muddy swamp, designated as the main commercial area by Raffles who began the trend of changing Singapore's shape by levelling a hill to form what is now Raffles Place and using the earth to fill in Boat Quay.

This stretch of river then became the centre of trade, where cargo boats were loaded and unloaded by coolies. These Chinese immigrants, engaged by a *towkay* or agent, would arrive here and work to pay off their passage to the *kongsi* which is rather like a company or clan. The immigrants worked as labourers, living in bachelor quarters until they had saved enough money to bring their wives and children from China. Street vendors abounded and food was often served by itinerant hawkers with meals eaten by customers squatting in the streets. Shophouses and godowns for Chinese and European traders were built further along the river bank but many men lived on their boats, which were anchored cheek by jowl.

Look at the lovely facades of the buildings at **Boat Quay**, now restored and housing an enticing selection of lunch spots, from Mc-Donalds for fastfood lovers to pasta and sandwich places. The river

bank is lined with various speciality Asian and Western restaurants, including many cosy pub and bars. Highly recommended is **Kinara** (tel: 533-0412), which serves delectable North Indian dishes in an exquisite setting filled with antiques from India. This peaceful waterside is a haven from the bustling city and offers a pleasant interlude from a hectic day. At night, Boat Quay attracts a sizeable crowd of locals as well as tourists who are lured by its riverside dining and drinking (see Itinerary 21 *Pick & Mix*).

Colourful Chinatown streets

After lunch, plunge into **Chinatown** down Canton Street, turning right at **Circular Road** where dingy shops sell bales of material. At the corner coffee shop make a sharp left turn down **Lorong Telok** passing the rattan shop filled with baskets of all shapes and sizes. Go left again into **North Canal Road** where you will find Chinese housewives buying dried food of every description, from sharks' fins and birds' nests to sea cucumbers. Perhaps you'd like some nuts, ginseng or Chinese tea to take home?

Cross over to the **OCBC Centre** where a sculpture by Henry Moore reclines, and bear left until Phillip Street, where you'll see the elaborately carved roof of the **Wak Hai Cheng Bio Temple**. Built in the 1850s, its heavy doors lead into a dark interior with intricately carved beams. Here, sunlight filters through smoke from the incense coils, brightening the fruit-laden altars.

Before wending your way to the Orchard Road area, walk through Chinatown to **People's Park**. This shopping centre is full of all sorts of interesting things, especially for the avid seamstress; fabrics from denim to the finest silks are sold at the lowest prices here – you'll have to bargain hard though. To get there, turn right at Church Street, left into China Street (passing **Far East Square** on your left – see Itinerary 1 *Pick & Mix*) and follow through to Cross Street. Just wandering through these little streets is a fascinating experience as you look into dark shops selling all kinds of goods. Turn right and pass South Bridge Road, then New Bridge Road. There you will find People's Park, both the centre and complex, where you can browse for hours.

Once you're done, take a taxi to **Goodwood Park Hotel** for high tea. Or take the MRT from **Outram Park** station. Go down Eu Tong Sen Street, past People's Park Complex and Pearl's Centre, turning right before Cantonment Road. At **Orchard** station, take the underpass to Tangs, then head towards Far East Plaza. Goodwood Park Hotel is just beyond.

Located along Scotts Road, this hotel with its distinctive tower was the Teutonia Club before World War I. A traditional English tea is served from 2.30–6.30pm at **Cafe L' Espresso** (tel: 737-7411), albeit buffet style, where you can choose from a wide selection of different teas, sandwiches, scones and cakes. Light, soothing music is played for you as you relax and recover from the rigours of sightseeing.

Thus fortified, get ready for some of the best shopping this side of the equator. Walk down Scotts Road. On your left is the

Orchard Road skyline

huge **Far East Plaza**. Past the Hyatt Regency is the ritzy **Scotts**, which has an excellent range of silks and garments at the China Silk House and other boutiques to tempt you.

Directly opposite is another shopping mall, the **Pacific Plaza** with Tower Records as its anchor tenant. Just next door, at the intersection with Orchard Road, is **Shaw Centre**, home to a branch of the Japanese department store **Isetan**. Facing Shaw Centre on Orchard Road is the imposing glass and steel building of **Wheelock Place**. Borders, the giant American bookstore chain, occupies the whole of the ground floor. Watch your step at Borders though; you may just trip over one of many inert bodies sprawled over the aisles taking advantage of its liberal book browsing policy.

At the junction of Scotts and Orchard roads, next to the Marriot hotel, is the well-known **Tang's** department store. Its original owner CK Tang arrived in Singapore in 1922 and was the first trader to recognise the potential of Orchard Road, now, of course, the main shopping street in Singapore. Being a Christian, the former Chinese cemetery opposite this site did not bother him. His

business flourished and outgrew its original building and is now a spacious department store selling everything from Chinese artifacts to household items, clothes, jewellery, watches and electronics.

By now, if you're sufficiently fatigued, Orchard Road will seem like a blur of malls stretching mercilessly into the horizon. If not, continue your walk down Orchard Road, past **Lucky Plaza**, the **Promenade** and the **Paragon** shopping malls. On the other side of the road is striking blue-panelled **Wisma Atria**; just next to it, the mammoth **Ngee Ann City**, with its equally large Japanese-run **Takashimaya** department store. By the time you pass the **Heeren** (with its bustling outdoor Spinelli's coffee shop), **Emerald Mall** and reach the lovely old pastel houses of **Peranakan Place** in Emerald Hill Road, you'll know the meaning of our adage: that in Singapore you can shop until you drop. Literally.

Shopping fiends will want to continue to **Robinson's** department store next door at **Centrepoint**, along with an enormous selection of other shops. In **Cuppage Road**, just around the corner, are galleries and shops selling wares from all over Asia. Mere mortals will definitely need a drink by now. At Peranakan Place, there is an outdoor pub and restaurant called **Papa Joe's Outdoors** or you can pop indoors to **Esmirada** (tel: 735-3476), a Mediterranean restaurant and wine cellar. **Papa Joe's Cantina Bar** upstairs features top international bands nightly. Everything stays open late so you can explore this part of town till you're tired. You'll also find **Que Pasa** (tel: 235-6626), a Peranakan house transformed into a wine bar, sandwiched in between two others pubs, **No. 5** and **Ice Cold Beer**. For jazz fans, **The Saxophone** in Cuppage Road is highly recommended.

Drink el fresco at Peranakan Place

Temples and Traditional Crafts

Start off at a local market, then enjoy an Indian breakfast before a stroll around a Hindu temple and two very different Chinese temples. Lunch in Kampong Glam, followed by an afternoon browse in Arab Street where you will visit Sultan mosque, and then to Thieves Market in Sungei Road. Spend the evening at Suntec City or Marina Square.

Today you'll visit places of worship of the three main communities of Singapore: Indian, Chinese and Malay. You'll see a fascinating Hindu temple, followed by two very different Chinese temples which combine Buddhism and Taoism (with a little ancestral worship thrown in for good measure), and dur-

Temple guardians

ing the afternoon a Malay mosque. Along the way browse through shops selling traditional wares and see how the local people live and work.

Ethnic enclaves in Singapore are the exception rather than the norm. Although a few areas are predominantly the domain of one or the other main racial groups – such as Little India, Chinatown and the Malay area of Kampong Glam – generally, all over the island, the different races live and worship in close proximity. In Little India, for instance, you will find Indian and Chinese temples standing literally side by side. This area is described in greater detail in Itinerary 2, *Pick & Mix*, so it's a good idea to read that section, then choose how much you want to see on this day.

A magnet for the Indian minority community, Serangoon Road attracts droves of Indian migrant workers who work in Singapore's construction industry on weekend nights. If crowds bother you, stay away during these times. As a mosque visit is included today, please dress appropriately – no shorts or sleeveless tops, and women, especially, should avoid tight or revealing clothes.

Begin before breakfast by taking a taxi to **Serangoon Road**, to what is locally known as KK or **Kandang Kerbau** market, meaning 'Buffalo Pen' in Malay. In the old days this was indeed a cattle market. It is still the site of a fascinating 'wet' market selling live chickens and all kinds of meat and fish. There is a myriad of

31

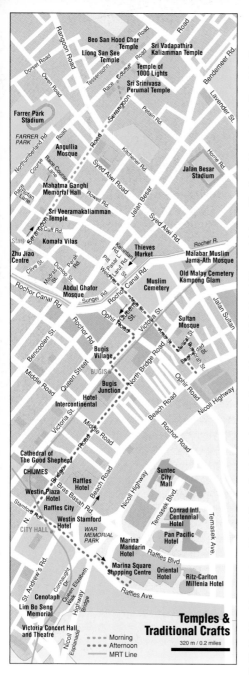

Map labels:

Dorset Road
Owen Road
Rangoon Road
Beo San Hood Chor Temple
Liong San See Temple
Sri Vadapathira Kaliamman Temple
Road
Temple of 1000 Lights
Sri Srinivasa Perumal Temple
Tessensohn Rd.
Race Course Road
Bendemeer Rd.
Lavender St.
Petain Rd.
Farrer Park Stadium
FARRER PARK
Serangoon Road
Northumberland Rd.
Angullia Mosque
Race Course Lane
Kitchener Rd.
Syed Alwi Road
Horne Rd.
Jalan Besar Stadium
Mahatma Ganghi Memorial Hall
Rowell Rd.
Jalan Besar
Sri Veeramakaliamman Temple
Syed Alwi Rd.
Cuff Rd.
Serangoon
Komala Vilas
Thieves Market
Kelantan Ln.
Rocher R.
Zhu Jiao Centre
Clive St.
Perak Rd.
Dunlop St.
Pitt St.
Prasat St.
Larut Rd.
Weld Rd.
Malabar Muslim Jama-Ath Mosque
Old Malay Cemetery
Kampong Glam
Madras St.
Abdul Ghafor Mosque
Sungei Rd.
Rochor Canal Rd.
Muslim Cemetery
Rochor Canal Rd.
Bencoolen St.
Rochor Rd.
Ophir Road
Queen St.
Victoria St.
Sultan Mosque
Jalan Sultan
Middle Road
Queen Street
Bugis Village
BUGIS
North Bridge Road
Bugis Junction
Ophir Road
Victoria St.
Hotel Intercontinental
Middle Road
Beach Road
Rochor Road
Nicoll Highway
Cathedral of The Good Shepherd
CHIJMES
Bras Basah Rd.
Suntec City Mall
Westin Plaza Hotel
Raffles Hotel
Beach Road
Stamford Rd.
Raffles City
Temasek Blvd.
Conrad Intl. Centennial Hotel
Westin Stamford Hotel
CITY HALL
WAR MEMORIAL PARK
Pan Pacific Hotel
Nicoll Highway
Marina Mandarin Hotel
Raffles Blvd.
Temasek Ave.
St. Andrew's Rd.
Connaught Dr.
Queen Elizabeth Walk
Nicoll Highway
Esplanade Bridge
Cenotaph
Lim Bo Seng Memorial
Victoria Concert Hall and Theatre
Marina Square Shopping Centre
Oriental Hotel
Ritz-Carlton Millenia Hotel
Raffles Ave.

Temples & Traditional Crafts
320 m / 0.2 miles
- - - Morning
••• Afternoon
— MRT Line

---

colourful stalls where you'll find exotic fruits and vegetables. Singaporeans of all races come here to buy spices and foodstuffs for every type of Asian cuisine.

The official name of the market, though rarely heard, is **Zhu Jiao Centre**. Later in the day a variety of stalls upstairs will open for business.

Cross Serangoon Road and you'll feel as if you have been transported straight to Delhi. Pungent spices will assail your nostrils, loud music and car horns blast in your ears and a riot of colours will surround you. The entire area presents wonderful photo opportunities with Indian women looking resplendent in their brightly coloured *saris*, and the men dapper in their traditional Indian *dhoti* or local check-patterned *sarong* (literally 'tube' in Malay). Trishaws wobble and weave in and out of traffic, in the old days delivering piles of washing and provisions or taking women home from the market, but these days more likely to be playing host to gawking tourists.

You might like to explore this part of Little India first by visiting **Little India Arcade**, across the road. You'll find an air-conditioned food court that specialises in, naturally, Indian food. Outside the food court and across the street are shops selling Indian jewellery, souvenirs, crafts, clothes and accessories. Good buys are Indian silks, sold in *sari* lengths of 5½m (18ft) and costing from S$30 to well over S$500 for exquisite materials embroidered with gold and silver thread.

Along Serangoon Road are also numerous provision

Indian fortune-teller

shops selling flour, rice, spices, cooking utensils and everything a cook needs for Indian cooking.

Further along, at a tiny roadside stall, a vendor makes *pan* by wrapping up areca nut, gambier, tobacco and a little lime in *seray* (betelnut leaf). This mixture, which is chewed (and later spat out onto the streets much to the dismay of the local health authorities) by Indians and Malays, supposedly aids digestion and promotes potency.

On some days, you may chance upon the itinerant street fortune-teller outside the Komala Vilas restaurant. If so, don't miss having your fortune told by the green parakeet, who will pick out your fortune card for S$1. Then, go into the air-conditioned cool of **Komala Vilas**, noisy and always full downstairs but calmer upstairs. It's time to savour a crispy 50-cm long *dosai* or pancake made of rice and gram flour, which makes the most delicious breakfast for about S$2. Local coffee sweetened with condensed milk is the usual accompaniment. You may enjoy browsing in the jewellery shops next door where rows and rows of gleaming yellow gold necklaces, rings, anklets and bracelets twinkle enticingly. All are sold according to weight, with the current prices for 22K gold prominently displayed. Older Singaporeans swear by 22K gold and eschew anything less pure than that.

As you leave, turn right and walk up the road (about a 20-minute walk), or take a taxi or bus to Sri Srinivasa Perumal Temple. Either way, on Belilios Road on the left, you will pass the ornately carved and brightly painted entrance or *gopuram* of the **Sri Veerakaliamman Temple**. Here, Kali, the consort of Shiva – one of the three main Hindu deities – is worshipped with fervour.

Further along Serangoon Road you will see Muslims praying at the **Angullia Mosque**. This mosque was built over 100 years ago, but has since been renovated. A few metres away is another wonderful *gopuram*. Rising to a height of over 21m (70ft), this is the entrance to the **Sri Srinivasa Perumal Temple**. This elaborately decorated mid-19th century temple was almost completely rebuilt in the 1960s and the enormous *gopuram* added 10 years later by craftsmen from South India. The funding was largely raised by a prominent local Indian philantrophist P Govindasamy Pillai, whose family owns several shops in Little India.

The figures on the *gopuram* depict the various incarnations of Vishnu, also known as Perumal, the Preserver of Life, who appears on earth from

Roof detail of a Hindu temple

time to time in different forms and to whom the temple is dedicated. If lucky enough, you might hear the beating of drums heralding a procession of devotees led by the priest, followed by women with fragrant jasmine in their hair and carrying offerings.

It is from here that the Thaipusam procession begins, either in January or February each year and ending at Chettiar Temple in Tank Road. Devotees who have prepared themselves by fasting pierce their tongues, cheeks and bodies with spikes and skewers – all without shedding a drop of blood – to support their *kavadi*, which are great arched steel structures decorated with peacock feathers. These acts of faith are performed either as penance or gratitude to Lord Murugan, Shiva's son. The great procession is an awesome sight and a must-see if you're in Singapore during this time.

Leave the temple and to your left you will see a path through a HDB (Housing Development Board) estate. These flats are typical of the subsidised housing provided by the Singapore government, in which almost 90 percent of the population now live. Colourful washing flutters on poles suspended from the windows while plants, caged birds and Chinese lanterns brighten up the balconies.

Out on Race Course Road, turn right, and you will come to the Chinese **Temple of 1000 Lights**, so called because the 15-m (50-ft) high statue of the Buddha is surrounded by that exact number of light bulbs, if you can be bothered to count. Just inside the door is part of a branch of the sacred Bodhi tree under which the Buddha is said to have attained enlightenment. There is also an enlargement of the Buddha's footprint, inlaid with mother-of-pearl.

All around the base of the great figure are windows where

The Buddha in the Temple of 1000 lights

colourful figures depict scenes from the life of the Buddha. Follow the story round and enter the little room at the back where a figure of a reclining Buddha shows how he passed away from the earth.

Over the road are some lovely old houses and the Taoist **Liong San See Temple** with its wonderfully carved roof.

The temple is dedicated to Kuan Yin, the Goddess of Mercy, who has 18 arms to help all those in distress. Seated in front of her is a statue of the Buddha. Kuan Yin is a popular deity and you will often see people bowing fervently in prayer, holding incense sticks between the palms of their hands. The temple is peaceful, a haven of red and gold glowing in the flickering candle-light. The altar table is usually laden with fruit, and the air permeated with incense. Just above are intricately carved wooden beams. If you go through to the courtyard at the back, you will see hundreds of memorial tablets. There, relatives of the deceased pray for the souls of the departed.

Batik galore at Arab street

Back out in the fresh air, hail a taxi to Beach Road, which as its name suggests, was once the seashore. Stop at the corner of **Arab Street**, the Islamic area of Singapore. The history of this area, designated for Arabs and Malays by Raffles, is described in more detail in Itinerary 10, *Pick & Mix*.

Arab Street is full of traditional Islamic and Malay wares, such as prayer mats, black caps called *songkok*, lace caps for *Hajis* and *Hajas* (men and women who have made the pilgrimage to Mecca), copies of the Koran and even tambourines used in wedding ceremonies. But that's not all. It's also a cornucopia of *batik*, bangles, buttons, beads and baskets. You'll also find brilliantly coloured floral *sarong* lengths, wraparound skirts and patterned shirts. Go along **Baghdad Street** for shops filled chock-a-block with leather bags and shoes. Then, turn left at **Bussorah Street** for a perfect view of the golden-domed **Sultan Mosque** – the largest in Singapore – framed by delightful shophouses. If you're there at the right time, you might hear the *muezzin* calling the faithful to prayer from the minaret. If hunger gnaws at you, choose from any number of little coffeeshops and restaurants nearby.

As you leave, turn right and carry on browsing along Arab Street until you come to Rochor Canal Road, from where you cross over the canal to **Sungei Road**. Popularly called **Thieves' Market**, although there is no such sign, this is where vendors spread their wares all over the street. Here you can find anything from wallets to watches (the cheapest fakes in town), and if you really rummage through the junk, you might just discover an antique or two.

Then, go back over the canal and down Arab Street, turning right into Queen Street to Ophir Road. Turn left at Ophir Road and head down the road, making a right turn when you reach Victoria Street. Ahead of you is the famous **Bugis Street** development (don't look for an actual 'Bugis Street' sign because there isn't one), albeit a sanitised version of a former unofficial Singapore landmark. The transvestite shows are no longer staged, and the only thing remotely risqué about 'Bugis Street' today are the provocative shows staged by outrageous cross-dresser and resident funnyperson Kumar at the **Boom Boom Room** (tel: 338-8187). Curtains up at 10pm and 1am nightly and watch the house come down in laughter to female impersonation acts and comedy skits that poke fun of everything uniquely Singaporean. **Bugis Village**, with its restaurants, shops and *pasar malam* (night market), housed in restored pre-war shophouses, provide an old-world contrast to the modern buildings in the vicinity. Opposite, **Bugis Junction**, an airy and multi-tiered shopping centre, is anchored by Seiyu and Parco department stores with the Hotel Intercontinental at one end. As usual, restaurants and shops abound.

The next stop is City Hall, either by MRT from Bugis Station, taxi or on foot. Walkers should make their way down Malabar Street, turn left, then turn right into North Bridge Road which will lead to the back of the Westin Stamford.

If you fancy a touch of the new, explore the sprawling **Suntec City**, Singapore's newest shopping, exhibition and convention centre. Here, you will find the oddly-named **Fountain of Wealth**. Resembling a gigantic brass space ship ready to take off, the fountain is noted in the Guinness Book as the world's largest. The **Conrad International** nearby provides convenient luxury accommodations for Suntec City conventioners. Adjacent is **Millennia Walk** with more shops and restaurants. Opposite is **Marina Square** shopping mall where three hotels, **The Oriental**, the **Marina Mandarin** and the **Pan Pacific** – each with a spacious atrium and linked by a shopping complex designed by the American architectural firm John Portman and Associates – stands on reclaimed land. The bubble lift creeping up the outside of the Pan Pacific Hotel offers the visitor with a strong stomach an impressive view of the harbour and city as you rise up from the pool of water below. Adjacent is the new six-star **Ritz-Carlton Millenia**, a hotel that looks far more impressive inside than out and with perhaps the finest harbour views in Singapore. Most of these hotels have bars and discos, so there's no need to hit the sack too early.

Right: a Thaipusam procession

Morning Itineraries

1. Chinatown

A walk through Chinatown, looking at temples and shopping at the quaint Tanjong Pagar area.

Start in the heart of old Singapore, where trade began in attap huts, flourished in narrow shophouses and continues today in gleaming high-rises. Take a taxi to the oldest Chinese temple in Singapore, the **Thian Hock Keng Temple** (Temple of Heavenly Bliss) in **Telok Ayer Street**. Before land reclamation in the 1880s, this was the seashore, and it was here that newly-arrived immigrants erected a temple to thank Ma-Zu-Po, the Goddess of the Sea. Inside the temple, her statue, brought from Amoy, China, in 1840, still stands – between the God of Prosperity and the God of Health. The temple, which was recently restored, was completed in 1842 by craftsmen using materials from China and without a single nail.

Dragons, for the Chinese, are divine creatures, not the symbol of evil they represent in the west. Here, they chase the central flame of immortality on the roof of the temple and wind their way around solid granite columns. Buddhists and Taoists worship here amidst

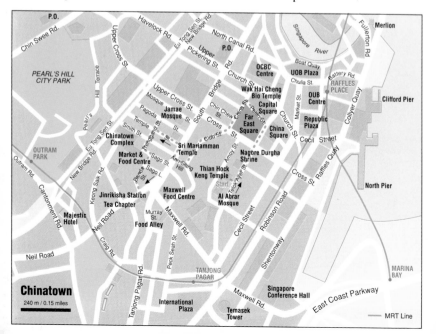

Chinatown just before the Lunar New Year

spirals of incense smoke and altars piled high with offerings of fruit. Door gods and stone lions guard the entrance.

Telok Ayer Street was once the most important street in Singapore, as evidenced by the many religious buildings and clan associations which formed a nexus for the early immigrant community.

Turn left outside the temple and look up to see the juxtaposition of old and new which typifies Singapore. High above the old shophouses the city buildings rise into the sky.

Turn left and walk pass a tiny park on the left to the **Nagore Durgha Shrine**, also known as the Masjid Chulia. Read the plaque on the wall and then peep in. The outside is of an interesting style, with classical columns supporting the Indian influenced upper floor.

Continue up Telok Ayer Street and pass Cross Street where a whole street block bordered by Pekin and China streets has been transformed into the **Far East Square**. Comprising retail outlets and restaurants in restored shophouses, this is an attempt to recreate the Chinatown of yesteryear. Especially interesting is the **Fu Tak Chi Museum** (open daily 10am–10pm) at 76 Telok Ayer Street, which displays more than 200 artifacts from old Chinatown, including bowls, plaques and birth certificates. Just opposite is the mammoth **China Square** food court and on the top floor is the funky **House of Mao** restaurant which serves Hunanese cuisine amid kitschy Mao memorabilia.

Turn left into Pekin and China streets and pass Cross Street again into **Club Street**, perhaps taking a few moments to rummage through the wares offered in the street alley on the right. A 'Thieves Market' comes to life here in the afternoons and bargain hunters will find many old,

Chinatown street scene

39

Gaily decorated to catch the eye

but not-quite-antique-yet items, from old coins, records and semi-precious gemstones to discarded household items. Memorabilia collectors should have a ball at this 'five-foot way' (pavement) junk store. Walk through Club Street, past the makeshift barber shop on the street and cross to the right to look at the pretty facade of No. 40. Unlike the smartly restored offices and restaurant-cafes, the front of this antique-junk store has not changed for the last few decades. As you stand under the front door, look up at the peephole, through which the residents above observe prospective visitors below. Club Street and the adjacent Mohammad Ali Lane are full of fashionable eating places like **Gaetano** and **Da Paolo** Italian restaurants and **Clips Wine Bar**. The road bends right into **Ann Siang Hill**, pass **Beaujolais** bar, a favourite watering hole for expats in Singapore.

Sizzling barbecued pork slices, anyone?

When you reach South Bridge Road, cross over and turn to your right. You'll see the twin towers of the **Jamae Mosque** and the ornamental *gopuram* over the entrance to the **Sri Mariamman** temple, the oldest Hindu temple in Singapore. It began as a wooden building in 1827 on this site, chosen for its proximity to water which is necessary for performing religious rites. The most important annual festival is that of Thimithi, a spectacular fire-walking ceremony held in July or August in honour of the Goddess Draupadi.

Turn right as you leave the temple into Temple Street and wander down to **Trengganu Street**. Walk past shops selling souvenirs as well as all kinds of dried foods, cakes and fish. Most interesting of all is the **Chinese medical hall** at the intersection of Temple and Terengganu streets, where all kinds of esoteric medicines are sold, from pearls (which the pharmacist will grind to a fine powder) to dried birds' nests, snakes and seahorses. These ingredients, when boiled into a soup for several hours, are believed to be beneficial to the health by the Chinese.

If you'd like to see a 'wet' market, **Chinatown Centre**, a modern building, is just at the corner of **Sago Street**. In the basement, vegetables and live snakes, frogs and turtles are sold (not as pets but for the pot). Along Sago Street are shops selling Chinese products. Go down **Banda Street** and you'll come to **Sago Lane**, once known as the Street of the Dead for its death houses, where the old and chronically sick would wait out their time. Today, the houses have been levelled and the land awaits development.

Following Banda Street, you will emerge at South Bridge Road again. Turn right and cross over to **Neil Road**. Now you are in **Tanjong Pagar** conservation area, a fascinating place to explore. You'll find everything from English pubs and Italian restaurants to relocated clog makers.

On the corner is the Jinrikisha Station, once the centre for these human-powered conveyances, but now **The China Town** seafood restaurant. Just across Tanjong Pagar Road is Maxwell Road, where you'll find **Food Alley**, filled with Asian restaurants. But first, a cup of tea. Find the **Tea Chapter** at 9A Neil Road, take off your shoes, go upstairs and let yourself be served Chinese tea in traditional style.

Tanjong Pagar shophouses

An experience of the Indian Subcontinent as you walk around the Serangoon Road area known as 'Little India'.

This itinerary was partially covered in *Day Two*, so you may wish to refer to this section for more details on some of the sights. Also, you might like a light snack before this walk, as it takes about half an hour to reach the coffeeshop where you have a late breakfast. Ask the taxi driver to take you to the corner of Serangoon Road and Rochor Canal Road where you'll see the **Zhu Jiao Centre**, a market and hawker centre more popularly known as *Tekkah*.

This area, although never officially designated for Indians, attracted them in the early years of this century because it was the centre of the brick and cattle industry. Indians, both free and convict labourers, were responsible for some of Singapore's most lovely

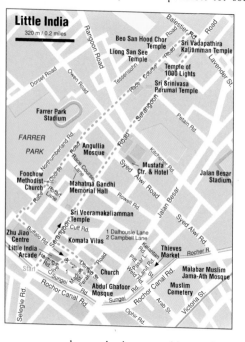

buildings, including St Andrew's Cathedral. Although there are no longer any kilns or cattle, 'Little India' remains alive with noise, colour and exotic aromas and is still the heart of the Indian community. Today, the area is also a meeting point for scores of Indian migrant workers, mainly from the construction industry, who gather there on weekend nights.

Little India is an attack on the senses. Amidst the multi-coloured flowers of the garland-maker, glittering gold jewellery in the shop window displays and bikes and trishaws winding in and out of the steady stream of cars, you'll see women festooned in bright silk *saris* and *dhoti*-clad men. Listen to the trishaw bells, car horns, brakes screeching and radios blaring out different Indian songs from all directions and you could be transported to India.

Escape from the bustle and the heat by entering the **Little India Arcade** at the corner of Serangoon Road and Hastings Road. Inside you will find an air-conditioned food court with many Indian food stalls. Outside, shops spill out onto the street with their exotic spices and brightly coloured merchandise. Aromatic powders of all colours from bright yellow turmeric to deep red chilli are piled high in sacks. Boxes spill over with cloves, cinnamon sticks, nutmegs, cardamom pods, black peppercorns and seeds of coriander, cumin, fennel and mustard. Outside are baskets full of onions,

Colourful garlands on sale in Little India

garlic, dried chillies, and dried fish and prawns of all shapes and sizes. *Pappadum*, pulses, rice, ghee, saffron – everything you'll ever need to cook an Indian meal can be found in these provision stores.

Go past Dalhousie Lane (named after the Marquis of Dalhousie, Governor General of India from 1848–56), up Clive Street and Campbell Lane to **Madras Street**. The houses here have bright facades with coloured tiles and delicate tracery. Look out for mirrors above the doors which deflect evil, believed to travel in a straight line. At the end of Madras Street is Dunlop Street. Turn right and walk on until you reach the blue gates of the **Abdul Gafoor Mosque**. You'll enter an oasis of tranquillity, a little courtyard shaded by a fruit-laden mango tree. Steps lead up to the star-studded mosque with its gracefully curved arches and windows. In the houses opposite, surmounted with the star and crescent, both Indian and Malay Muslims quietly carry on with their lives while prayers and Islamic instruction take place inside the mosque.

Now it's time to join the locals for breakfast. Retrace your steps down Dunlop Street, and turn right into Perak Road. Join the schoolchildren and taxi drivers in the corner coffee shop. Not much English is spoken, but enough to understand your order.

You can order either from the Muslim stall or the Chinese noodle stall. Watch the Chinese stallholder dunk noodles of all shapes and sizes into a cauldron of boiling broth and expertly retrieve them to serve with prawns and vegetables. Order coffee, which will come sweet and laced with condensed milk unless you like it black, in which case you should order a *kopi-o*. Enjoy these local treats and then sit awhile and watch the backstreet life of 'Little India'.

Whimsical Madras Street facades

Tossing chapatis and pratas

After your break, wander on down Dunlop Street towards Serangoon Road, past **ASK & Sons,** one of the last butcher shops left here. Walk on past little roadside tailor shops and look at the *mamak* ('uncle' in Tamil) man's wares displayed in the hole-in-the-wall shop. He sells everything from tea to toothpaste, all packed into shallow shelves set in the wall. Dunlop Street is also full of Indian garment and textile shops. One of the oldest and most established is **Hanifa Textiles,** which sells a wide range of colourful Indian fabrics, in addition to competitively-priced electrical goods.

Back on Serangoon Road again, browse through the shops which you may have seen if you followed the *Day Two* itinerary. You'll see jewellers selling ornate 22K gold earrings, necklaces, bracelets and anklets. If you search the display shelves hard enough, you may find parts of the body or cobras crafted in silver for use in supplication at the temple. A motley assortment of pictures – India's late Prime Minister, Mrs Gandhi, Jesus, Indian deities and film stars – adorn walls and a pavement fortune-teller with a green parakeet waits patiently to pick out the card which tells your fortune for S$1.

Further along on the left at **Belilios Road** is the **Sri Veeramakaliamman Temple.** This Hindu temple is dedicated to Kali, consort to Shiva. Both deities are feared as well as loved, for they represent the elemental powers of the universe. Shiva's consort is known as Parvati in her benign form, but as Kali she is powerful and destructive, the manifestation of anger against evil. Her black statue is at the centre of the temple.

To the left of the temple, Kali is shown with her two sons,

Hindu devotees with hands clasped in prayer

Sri Veeramakaliamman Temple

Ganesh, the elephant god, and Murugan, the child god, who is sometimes depicted with four heads. At the back is the gory figure of Kali disemboweling her hapless victim. In the right hand corner of the hall are nine stones arranged in a square, representing the nine planets in the Hindu universe. Devotees circle this three times and stop in front of the planet which shows the day of their birth.

If you followed the *Day Two* itinerary, you may now prefer to explore this fascinating area on your own before making your way through to Race Course Road for lunch.

Otherwise, carry on up the road, making a brief foray up **Race Course Lane** to take a look at a bust of Mahatma Gandhi in the **Gandhi Memorial Hall**, the foundation stone of which was laid by Jawaharlal Nehru in 1950.

Before the junction of Serangoon Road and Kitchener Road, you'll come to **AB Mohamed Restaurant** where you'll see an Indian man slapping, pounding and folding a small mound of wheat flour dough before tossing it onto a hot griddle. This delicious Indian bread served with curry is called *roti prata*. Take a break here after the long walk and try this local snack.

A Little India vendor

Then, following the *Day Two* itinerary, walk up the road to the brightly coloured *gopuram* over the entrance to the **Sri Srinivasa Perumal Temple**. Instead of going straight to Race Course Road, continue up Serangoon Road to look at the **Sri Vadapathira Kaliamman Temple**. It is closed between noon and 4pm, so don't leave it too late to explore this other fascinating Hindu temple dedicated to Kali.

Liong San See Temple

Directly opposite the temple used to be a bird store. It is now a motorbike accessories shop but, coincidentally, the new tenant has two talkative parrots as mascots in front of the shop. Many Singaporeans keep birds as pets and will pay from S$20 to over S$1,000 for a cockatoo. Keeping songbirds is a traditional pastime and owners often gather in coffeeshops to watch their birds sing and compete with others. One such place, alive with birdsong in the mornings, is at the corner of Tiong Bahru and Seng Poh roads.*

At Balestier Road, turn left and sample some *tau sar pau*, steamed buns with red bean filling, each costing less than S$1, from the coffeeshop. Have the buns packed so you can munch them while walking, taking a left turn into **Race Course Road**.

Just along on the right is the small Chinese temple of **Beo San Hood Chor** where Kuan Yin, the Goddess of Mercy, is worshipped amidst red candles and incense sticks smoking in brass containers. If you peep round the back you may see old ladies relaxing in front of a TV. Further along on the right is the ornately decorated 80-year-old Chinese **Liong San See Temple**, which is described in the *Day Two* itinerary, as is the **Temple of 1000 Lights** across the road.

Continue walking past the flats on the right which have the modern day equivalent of the 'five-foot way' pavement – Raffles' idea seems to have proven extremely practical and long-lasting.

You may be wondering why there is no race course on a street named after it. Well, there used to be one just behind the low-rise estate on the right, where Farrer Park is today. Apart from being the venue for horse racing, this green expanse was where the first plane landed in 1911, and in 1919 the first flight from England to Australia made a stop here.

Way to heaven on the Temple of 1000 lights

Grab a trishaw to K K Market

Carry on down, past the Foochow Methodist Church. There in front of you is a row of the best South Indian restaurants (**Muthu's Curry** at the corner is a good bet) in Singapore. After all that walking, you'll be ready for a hot curry, eaten from a banana leaf (with your fingers) and an ice-cold beer or lime juice. After lunch, you might like to make your way over to the **Zhu Jiao Centre** and explore the stalls upstairs, where apart from clothing of all kinds, you will also find a fascinating collection of cheap brassware and luggage. There's much to see before your visit draws to a close.

3. Of Birds and Beasts

A day out in Jurong at the bird and reptile parks.

Make an early start to avoid the crowds and see the birds at the **Jurong Bird Park** (Monday to Friday 9am–6pm; Sunday and public holiday 8am–6pm, tel: 265-0022). Take a taxi from the city centre to the park, or the MRT to **Boon Lay** station, where you can board bus no. 194 or 251.

The 20-ha (49-acre) park is home to some 6,000 birds from 500 different species from all over the world. Acknowledged as one of the leading bird parks in the region and committed to avian preservation, the park attracts over a million visitors each year. When

Pretty flamingoes

you arrive, you will hear the calls of the birds even before you see them.

One of the first exhibits you'll see is the exciting Penguin Parade, where endearing penguins live and play in an environment similar to that of the South Pole. Marvel at how the birds seem to fly underwater and watch them feed at 10.30am and 3.30pm. The Fuji World of Hawks show – featuring eagles, falcons, owls and the magnificent condor – is at 10am over at the **Fuji Hawk Walk**. Later, you might like to look at the **Falconry Museum**. Another must-see is the All Stars Birdshow at the **Pools Amphitheatre** where you'll be thrilled by the likes of toucans catching balls and flamingoes doing a Caribbean dance. The twice-daily show features over 100 birds and starts at 11am and 3pm.

Other fascinating bird shows throughout the morning include Hornbill Chit Chat at 11.45am at the Hornbill Exhibit and an audio-visual show on the Wonderful World of Birds at noon, 1pm and 2pm. With so many free shows included in your admission ticket, check the show times and plan your route accordingly.

After you have wandered around the array of exhibits – the stunning **Hornbill and Toucan Exhibit** is another must-see – enter the **World of Darkness** to catch a rare glimpse of nocturnal birds, or hop onto the **Panorail** for a close encounter of the feathered kind. Built at a cost of S$20 million, the elevated Panorail covers a

Scenes from the bird show

winding route of 1.7km (1 mile) and opens dramatic new horizons of the park. Visitors should have their noses pressed against the large windows for the ride into the **Waterfall Aviary**.

Around lunchtime, leave the bird park and cross the carpark to the **Jurong Reptile Park**, where you can lunch at the Jumbo Jurong Seafood Restaurant. The energetic might like to walk up the road behind the bird park to the **Jurong Hill Lookout Tower** for a view of Jurong port and the southern islands. There is a restaurant here serving Indonesian and Korean cuisine. Up on this hilltop is a park with trees planted by famous (some are now infamous) visitors to Singapore.

After lunch, go to the **Jurong Reptile Park** (open daily 9am–6pm, tel: 261-8866), and walk round the crocodile enclosures, never mind the smell. Apart from the crocs, there are also the **Snake Cavern** and **Living Dragons** enclosures. The latter features crocodile monitors and Malayan monitor lizards. Wander around the gardens and look at the piles of muddy-coloured pythons in their cages, and in solitary splendour, two golden pythons curled around the branches of their enclosure.

Feeding time (daily 10.30am and 5pm) is also a good time to watch the crocodiles in action, jumping up high for their food. You can browse around until it's official showtime. At 11.45am and 2pm daily, great crocodiles are heaved out of the water to be danced with and kissed (ugh!). After which time, you probably have had enough and want to take bus no. 194 or 251 back to Boon Lay MRT station for your connecting train back to the city.

4. Of Flora and Fauna

See a hillside covered with thousands of brightly-coloured orchids, then visit one of the most beautiful zoos in the world.

Get off to an early start by taxi from the city centre to the **Mandai Orchid Gardens** (open daily 8.30am–5.30pm, tel: 269-1036) in the north of the island. Ask the driver to take you via Upper Thomson Road, where you will drive through some of Singapore's peaceful but fast-disappearing rural countryside.

Enjoy the profusion of exotic blooms growing on gentle slopes and discover how orchids are grown in a mixture of charcoal

Colourful koi

and brick; then walk down to the peaceful Water Garden.

Singapore is a major exporter of orchids, and one of the most wonderful souvenirs you can buy here is a box of fresh orchids; with proper care the flowers will last for many weeks. A dozen sprays will cost about S$15. If you don't want to carry a box around, buy some at the airport just before you leave.

After that, take a 15-minute walk down the road to another attraction; the **Singapore Zoological Gardens** (open daily 8.30am–6pm, tel: 269-3411). Bordering Seletar Reservoir, in a glorious setting of secondary forest, the zoo covers 90ha (22 acres), 28 of which have been developed to display over 200 species of wildlife.

The zoo is often called 'the Open Zoo' as most of the animals are cleverly separated from people by water moats and other concealed or low-profile barriers to ensure an unobstructed view. The ani-

No cages for animals at the Singapore Zoological Gardens

mals are housed in creative enclosures very much like their natural habitats. Pygmy hippos wallow in their riverine environment while polar bears swim in an air-conditioned Arctic environment. Gibbons and spider monkeys leap through trees, and rhinos share space with antelopes in a stunning recreation of the African plains.

The zoo boasts the world's largest colony of orangutans, the result of a very successful breeding programme. The most famous of these creatures is Ah Meng, who takes tea with visitors at 4pm and is also up for breakfast at 9am. Call to make reservations. Animal shows featuring reptiles, primates, elephants and sea lions are staged several times a day at the open-air amphitheatre. Animal feeding times are posted at the zoo entrance, with the most spectacular feasts at the polar bear and lion enclosures.

Just alongside the zoo is the splendid **Night Safari Park** (open daily 7.30pm–midnight). Covering some 40ha (98 acres) of dense tropical rainforest, the park allows you to experience the nocturnal habits of wild animals in their natural habitats. Travelling by tram, you will see creatures like the Indian rhinoceros, striped hyena, golden jackal and the Cape buffalo. Altogether, some 1,200 animals of over 110 species roam the grounds of the park, unobtrusively lit so that the animals are not disturbed. Just as interesting is the different types of terrain you'll encounter, from recreations of Himalayan foothills to wild savanna grasslands. For the more adventurous, walking trails allow you to get closer to the animals not easily seen from the trams.

If you rather not find your own way to the zoo, make use of the convenient Zoo Express (tel: 481-0166) which arranges tickets and transportation to the Singapore Zoological Gardens and the Night Safari Park and back from major hotels in town.

5. Mixed Heritage

A walk which gives an insight into Singapore's cultural mix.

Start at about 10am, or an hour earlier if a visit to the **Istana** is possible on New Year's Day, Chinese New Year, Hari Raya and Deepavali (*see Calendar of Special Events*). Take a taxi to Mohamed Sultan Road, just off River Valley Road, and 200m (660ft) on the right you will see the **Hong San See Temple**, built in 1908. It is reminiscent of Thian Hock Keng Temple in Chinatown, but much more peaceful. There are similar elaborate carvings and stone columns. The main deity is Kok Seng Wang, the Lord of Benefice.

Cross River Valley Road, turn right, and browse in the antique shops as you make your way to Tank Road. On your left is the **Sri Thandayuthapani Temple**, usually known as the **Chettiar Temple**, as it was built by the Chettiar community in the 1850s, and rebuilt in 1984. The temple, dedicated to Murugan, is especially crowded during the annual Thaipusam Festival (in January/February) and Navarathiri (in October). It boasts 48 glass panel friezes, each etched with a Hindu deity.

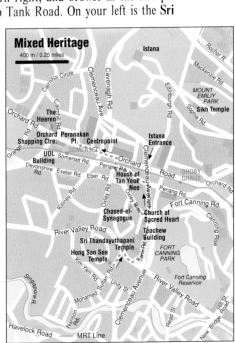

Leave the temple and turn left up towards Tank Road. Here, you'll see the **Teochew Building**, a curious blend of Chinese and western architectural influences.

Next door, make a brief halt at the **Church of the Sacred Heart**, designed by a French priest for Hakka and Cantonese speaking members of the Roman Catholic community. Continue up the road until you come to Oxley Rise, where you will see the off-white, classical **Chased-El Synagogue**. Retrace your steps to the intersection and take Clemenceau Avenue. At the corner of Penang Road is the former Salvation Army Headquarters. The building is interesting for its intricate architecture and the history behind it. It was once the town house of the wealthy Chinese merchant Tan Yeok Nee, built with granite columns and carvings from China in traditional Southern Chinese style. After a variety of owners, the Salvation Army acquired it in 1940. From 1942 to 1945,

The Chettiar Temple on Tank Road

the Japanese army took over it, and after the war the Salvation Army quietly repossessed it. The building has since been acquired by the government and awaits restoration.

From here you may see the white gates and uniformed guard of the **Istana** ('Palace' in Malay) which is the official residence of the President of Singapore. If open, it is well worth a visit.

Otherwise, continue to your left, under the shade of the angsana trees along Penang Road, turning right onto Orchard Road, where you walk along to your left until you reach the pastel buildings of **Peranakan Place** (see also *Day One* itinerary) on your right.

Cross the street and walk through the terrace cafe to the **Peranakan Showhouse Museum** on the right. It opens for guided tours from Monday to Friday at 3pm so leave yourself half an hour at least for a fascinating tour of a typical Peranakan house of the turn of the century. You'll learn the history of these Peranakans, also known as Straits Chinese, who settled in Malaya and intermarried with the Malays, creating their own unique culture.

The Peranakan language was a mixture of Malay and Chinese known as Baba Malay. The men are known as *baba*s and the women as *nonya*s, and although these days they are no longer a separate group, you can appreciate their culture through their decorative houses and their handiwork in intricate embroidery, lovely

porcelain, silverware and furniture. **Emerald Hill** is a charming little street, with interesting shops and restaurants, and wonderful old Peranakan-style houses to look at. **Katong** in the east of the island is another area where you will find houses of a similar style.

Peranakan Place Museum

Sentry at the main gate to the Istana

As to be expected in Singapore, the most popular vestige of these people is the Peranakan or *nonya* cuisine. A wonderful mixture of the influences of Malay, Chinese and Indian ways of cooking make this food eagerly sought after today.

There are plenty of places to have lunch here and in The Heeren and Centrepoint malls, and Cuppage Road beyond, so wander around and take your pick.

You're in the right area for an afternoon's shopping with an enormous selection of shops including Robinson's and St Michael's in Centrepoint. Cuppage Road is well worth exploring too, including the upper level of shops and galleries.

There's a wet market right at the end of Cuppage Road selling fresh fruit and flowers, as well as meat, fish and vegetables. The Cuppage Food Centre on the first floor is popular with the lunchtime office crowd. The selection of local food is wide and prices are cheap. This area is an interesting part of town and you may well decide to spend the whole afternoon here.

6. A Walk in the Jungle

Back in time, back to nature: the Bukit Timak Nature Reserve and Sungei Buloh Nature Park.

There's not much left in the way of jungle in Singapore, but it is still possible to spend a few hours walking through primary forest. The **Bukit Timah Nature Reserve** (tel: 470-9900) encompasses the highest hill on the island, but as it is only 162½m (534ft) above sea level, you won't need mountaineering skills to reach the summit.

This jungle is real, but rather too civilised, with dustbins, benches, man-made steps and even a tarred main road. It's a good idea to bring a bottle of water, a hand towel, mosquito repellent and antihistamine cream. Wear sensible shoes, of course. It is possible that you'll come across a scorpion, python or black cobra, but it's not very likely.

To get to the reserve at Hindhede Drive, off Bukit Timah Road, take a taxi, or alternatively make your way to **Newton** MRT station where you can board any of the following buses: SBS no. 170, 171 or TIBS no. 182.

At the entrance is the Visitor Centre, where you can buy a useful guide and drinks. A large map of the reserve is posted at the entrance, as well as at regular intervals during your walk.

The four indicated routes are marked in different colours, the

The route to exploring nature

yellow route being the longest, taking about 2½ hours to complete. The light blue walk takes about 1½ hours, the red less than an hour and the purple about 40 minutes. You can, of course, combine different coloured routes and explore the reserve as you like. From the summit you'll have a glorious view of Seletar Reservoir.

Traffic and the 20th century recede quickly as you set off up the path into the forest where little sunlight filters through the thick canopy of tropical rainforest. Keep your eyes open for interesting birds, insects, and small animals like squirrels and long-tailed macaques. If you see a lizard fly, it may be a flying dragon (draco), whose foldable gliding membrane enables it to glide up to 30m (99ft). Flowers are few and far between, but there are lots of interesting tropical trees and plants, like the insect-eating pitcher plant for instance.

Another interesting wildlife trek to tackle is the **Sungei Buloh Nature Park** (open daily 7am–7pm, tel: 794-1401) in the remote northwestern part of Singapore. To get there, take the MRT to **Kranji** station where bus no. 925 will take you to the park entrance on Sundays and public holidays. Otherwise, the bus will terminate at the Kranji Reservoir car park and you can take a 20-minute walk to the park entrance.

The 87-ha (215-acre) wetland nature reserve is an important stop for migratory birds along the East Asian Flyway and for this reason November is the best month for bird watching. The reserve

is remarkable for its amazing diversity of birdlife – an estimated 126 species of birds have been spotted so far. For visitors, observation hides carefully built among the mangrove swamps allow you to watch rare wildlife scenes and birds.

Sitting on the fence

A mighty triumvirate of museums: the Asian Civilisations Museum, Singapore History Museum and the Singapore Art Museum.

Start at the **Asian Civilisations Museum** (Tuesday, Thursday to Sunday 9am–5.30pm, Wednesday 9am–9pm, free guided tours at 11am and 2pm, tel: 338-0000) on Armenian Street, housed in the beautifully restored Tao Nan School. Concentrating on Chinese culture and civilisation, the museum houses a good selection of Chinese ceramics, jade, furniture and works of art. Multimedia presentations add an interesting visual dimension to the exhibits.

Turn left out of the museum and left into Stamford Road where you will see a splendid classical building surmounted by a gleaming dome. The **Singapore History Museum** (Tuesday, Thursday to Sunday 9am–5.30pm, Wednesday 9am–9pm, free guided tours at 11am and 2pm, tel: 375-2510) was designed by Major JF McNair, and originally opened in Queen Victoria's Jubilee Year. Singapore's early days are recreated in illuminated dioramas; recorded commentaries explain the cultural heritage of the island, and numerous collections and exhibits recreate the colonial, immigrant and Japanese periods in Singapore's history.

Cross Stamford Road and turn right into Bras Basah Road, where the **Singapore Art Museum** (Tuesday, Thursday to Sunday 9am–5.30pm, Wednesday 9am–9pm, free guided tours at 11am and 2pm, tel: 332-3222) stands. Housed in the former mission school, the venerable St Joseph's Institution, the 19th century structure is a fine example of sensitive restoration. Apart from the impressive permanent collection of some 4,000 Southeast Asian traditional and contemporary art, the museum also showcases special touring exhibits from time to time.

If your feet give way by now, the **Dome Cafe** adjacent to the museum serves wonderful sandwiches and freshly-brewed coffee.

The neo-classical Singapore History Museum building

Enter the dragon at Haw Par Villa Tiger Balm Gardens

8. Haw Par Villa Tiger Balm Gardens

Gaudy and grotesque recreations of hell, earth and heaven at a Chinese mythological theme park.

For a truly different experience, visit the **Haw Par Villa Tiger Balm Gardens** (open daily 9am–6pm, tel: 774-0300) at Pasir Panjang Road in the west of the island. To get to there, take the MRT to **Clementi** station, where you connect with SBS bus no. 10, or alight at **Buona Vista** MRT station and take bus no. 200.

This was originally the home of the well-known Aw family whose claim to fame rests on Tiger Balm, a herbal ointment used to cure everything from aches and pains to nausea. In 1986, the estate was turned into the Haw Par Villa Dragon World. Billed as the world's first high-tech Chinese mythological theme park, the attraction, complete with roller coaster-like rides, never quite took off. The rides have ground to a standstill and the Tiger Balm name has returned, no doubt because of its exotic association, but what is still fascinating here are the grotesque recreations of Chinese mythological hell.

Billed as the **Ten Courts of Hell**, the exhibit depicts all manner of torture in the nether world. Some are truly stomach-turning: evil-doers getting disembowelled and boiled in hot oil, impaled on spikes or sliced into two are just few of the more graphic scenes.

Afternoon Itineraries

9. Historical Hike

From museums to memorials, up Forbidden Hill and down the Singapore River on the trail of Singapore's past.

Lovers of fine architecture will appreciate the elegantly restored **Asian Civilisations Museum** (Tuesday, Thursday to Sunday 9am–5.30pm, Wednesday 9am–9pm, tel: 338-8500; see also Itinerary 7, *Pick & Mix*) on Armenian Street. Next door is **The Substation**, an arts centre which holds regular fringe-type plays and exhibitions. Near the junction of Armenian Street and Stamford Road is **The National Museum Shop** (Tuesday to Sunday 9.30am–6.30pm). Photographs and reproduction paintings of Singapore's past, Asian fabrics, porcelain, shadow play puppets, postcards and books on Asian history and culture are just some of the good buys here.

Across Stamford Road is MPH, another example of a beautifully restored building. Although the acronym stands for Malaysia Publishing House, the building started out life as the Methodist Publishing House back in 1908, printing bibles and Christian literature in English and ethnic languages for missionaries working in Asia.

Originally designed by architectural firm Swan & Maclaren, the building is a fine example of Edwardian street architecture, with a facade of Italian cinquecento and bold baroque arches. For years the red brick and plaster building was a prominent landmark. In 1990, the interior of the building was demolished except for the facade which, thankfully, has been preserved. Inside, the elegant wood-panelled interior holds four levels of books and information resources plus a music store.

Leave the MPH Building, turn right and continue along Stamford Road and right into Hill Street, passing the **Singapore Chinese**

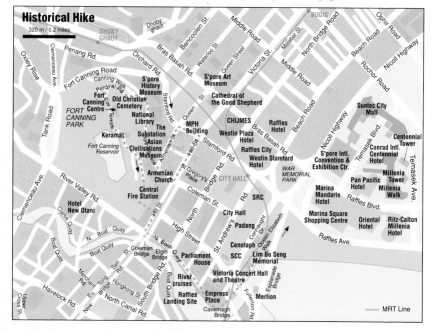

Historical Hike

320 m / 0.2 miles

MRT Line

The Armenian Church

Chamber of Commerce Building on your left. Built in 1966, it has two huge lions guarding each side of a blood-red, brass-studded door. Behind the guardians, carved into the walls are 18 colourful dragons. Further up Hill Street on the right is the **Armenian Church, Saint Gregory the Illuminator**, the oldest church in Singapore. Completed in 1837, it was designed by George Drumgold Coleman, and may have been inspired by St Martin-in-the-Fields in London, as well as its mother church in Erevan.

GD Coleman, an Irish architect, first came to Singapore in 1822, having worked in India and Batavia (Jakarta). Having designed and built the *attap*-roofed Residency on Fort Canning Hill for Sir Stamford Raffles, he went on to design other major government buildings, mansions and godowns in the neo-classical style (described more fully in the *Day One* itinerary).

Walk around the churchyard and pause at the gravestone of Agnes Joaquim, who created the national flower, the *Vanda Miss Joaquim*, a large purple hybrid orchid. Here, too, lie the Sarkies brothers who established Raffles Hotel in 1887.

At the exit, turn right into Coleman Street, where you can find out more about Singapore history through stamps at the **Singapore Philatelic Museum** (Tuesday to Sunday 9am–4.30pm). Coleman Street leads on to Canning Rise and on your way there is the **National Archives of Singapore** (Monday to Friday 9am–5pm, Saturday 9am–1pm, tel: 332-7911). On the first floor is a small poster exhibition of Singapore's modern history and the Archives Reference Room.

Further up Canning Rise is the white gateway of **Fort Canning**

The stately Raffles Hotel

59

Park. By the time Raffles arrived in Singapore in 1819, this hill was known as Bukit Larangan (Forbidden Hill) as it was rumoured to be haunted by spirits of Javanese princes who ruled from here in the 14th century. The last of these five rulers, Iskandar Shah, Prince of Palembang, is said to be buried here, although there is some doubt as to whether his remains at the **keramat** (shrine) are indeed in the tomb which may be seen today.

Raffles, undeterred by superstition or spirits, erected Coleman's wood and *attap* house up on the hill which was later renamed Government Hill. He also founded the first botanical gardens here, planting cocoa and spices, but this was closed in 1829.

In 1857, the military took over, building Fort Canning which was completed in 1860. This was an unqualified disaster as the enemy ships at sea were out of range of the guns, which if fired would have destroyed the town instead. The guns did serve, however, to announce the time at noon, dawn and dusk. The fort was demolished in 1907 and the hilltop is now a reservoir.

Through the gateway you will reach the first Christian cemetery in Singapore, great big gravestones huddled in a corner. Follow the path through a similar gateway to the ASEAN (Association of Southeast Asian Nations) sculpture garden. Keep going straight unless you wish to branch off to see the tombstones. Look out for a small bunker where General Percival, commander of the British forces, is said to have decided on the surrender of Singapore after the Japanese had cut off the island's water supply in February 1942.

Go past remnants of the wall and through the old fort. The bunker called the **Battle Box** (Tuesday to Sunday 10am–6pm, tel: 333-0510) is the island's largest underground military operations complex and part of the Malaya Command Headquarters during World War II. Animatronic figurines as well as realistic audio and video effects are used to bring you back to the day Singapore fell to the

Cruising down Singapore River

Japanese. There is a half-hour guided tour, following which you can explore the underground maze of tunnels and rooms.

Follow Cox Terrace till it leads you to a flight of stairs down to the former Hill Street Police Station. Continue walking downriver along North Boat Quay under the Coleman Bridge. Gone are the old bumboats which used to ply between the ships in the harbour and the godowns on the river bank. On the opposite bank the renovated shophouses of **Boat Quay** are home to restaurants and offices.

At the little kiosk just past Coleman Bridge, buy a ticket for a half-hour river cruise. The boats leave roughly every 20 minutes with a recorded commentary given on board. Take a ride upriver to **Clarke Quay**, popular for evening drinks and dinner, then out to Marina Bay to take in views of Singapore's commercial district.

Back on land, make your way along North Boat Quay, past Raffles' statue at the point he first landed in 1819 to the riverside terrace of the green and white Empress Place Building, which will open in 2000 as an extension of the Asian Civilisations Museum. Beyond Empress Place is Cavenagh Bridge with the Victoria Memorial Hall and Theatre on the left. Take the underpass to Queen Elizabeth Walk in Esplanade Park with the symbol of Singapore, the Merlion, on your right. On your left across the Padang are the colonial buildings of the Supreme Court, City Hall and St Andrew's Cathedral all described in the *Day One* itinerary.

You'll pass the **Lim Bo Seng Memorial**. During World War II, he was a resistance leader of Force 136 in Malaya and was brutally tortured to death by the Japanese. Further on is the **Cenotaph**, a memorial to Singapore men killed in World War I, with the names of the World War II dead added later. This was unveiled in 1922 by the Prince of Wales, later the Duke of Windsor. He was accompanied by Lord Mountbatten, who returned in 1945 as Supreme Allied Commander Southeast Asia to accept the surrender of the Japanese. Across Stamford Road you'll see four tapering pillars of the **War Memorial**, locally known as the 'Chopsticks', which symbolise the civilians of the four main racial groups who died at the hands of the Japanese during World War II.

By now you'll have gained a deeper understanding of how Singapore became what it is today. To round off the evening, leave the memorial by walking down Bras Basah Road, past Raffles Hotel on your right till you come to **CHIJMES** at the junction of Bras Basah Road and Victoria Street. Originally built in 1850s as the Convent of The Holy Infant Jesus, it underwent extensive renovations to re-open in 1995 as CHIJMES (pronounced *chimes*) an upscale retail, food and beverage, and arts complex.

One can dine as well as watch performances in its open Fountain Court. Performances are also held at the historic Chijmes Hall. The former chapel still retains much of its original beautiful 19th century stained-glass windows and intricate column capitals and is a popular venue for weddings. Within the walls of the restored neo-classical and gothic-styled buildings are ample courtyards and long covered walkways. There are souvenir shops, art galleries and a selection of restaurants as well as the trendy **Bon Sante** wine bar, making it a great place to dine and round off the heritage trail.

Singapore River at sunset

Malabar Muslim Jama-Ath Mosque

10. Kampong Glam

A walk around the Malay part of town, looking at mosques and a treasure trove of batik, baskets, bangles and beads.

Take a taxi to the corner of **Beach Road** and **Arab Street**. Don't forget to be appropriately dressed if you wish to enter the mosques. Avoid revealing clothes, sleeveless tops, shorts or short skirts.

This area of **Kampong Glam** was designated by Sir Stamford Raffles for Arabs and Muslims. The name is derived from 'Kampong' which means village in Malay, and the 'Glam' tree, the *Melaleuca Leucadendron*, with spirally arranged, narrow leaves and white flowers. The bark was prized for its medicinal values, and was also used by the Bugis and Malays to caulk their ships. The shophouses are as designated by Raffles, with the 'five-foot way' pavement for shelter; now a handy extension to the shops and a boon to people walking in the heat.

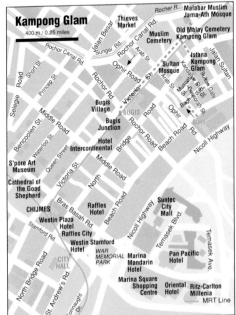

You'll find the best selection of rattan and basketware right on the corner. Further along are kaftans and sarongs and wonderful leather goods, as well as lace, tablecloths and prayer mats. Whatever you buy here will be cheaper than

Sultan Mosque

in shops in Orchard Road, and you can bargain.

Turn right into Baghdad Street, then left into **Bussorah Street.** Four weeks before the Muslim celebration of Hari Raya Puasa, this street spills over with vendors selling all kinds of delicacies for Muslims breaking their mandatory fast. From here, you will have a magnificent view of the golden-domed **Sultan Mosque.** Designed by the colonial architectural firm of Swan and Maclaren, the mosque – the largest in Singapore – was completed in 1928 and is one of over 80 mosques on the island. You might hear the muezzin calling the faithful at prayer time. Go inside and enjoy the feel of the soft, plush carpet donated by Saudi Arabia. Upstairs is where the women remain during worship.

At the exit, turn left and make your way to the old yellowish house ahead, going along Kandahar Street, with its lovely old pastel buildings, left onto Baghdad Street and then left again at the junction of Baghdad Street and Sultan Gate.

You will then come to the **Istana Kampong Glam.** Built in the early 1840s and now fallen into a state of disrepair, this building was once the palace of Sultan Ali Iskandar Shah, son of the first sultan of Singapore, Sultan Hussein. It was he, together with Temenggong Daeng Ibrahim, who ceded Singapore to the British East India Company for the princely sum of 5,000 Spanish dollars a year, plus this compound.

You can't go in, unfortunately, as the place is still lived in by descendants of the Sultan, so just take the alleyway on the right of the Istana out onto North Bridge Road.

Cross over and take Jalan Kubor through to Victoria Street. Turn right on Victoria Street and there at the corner is the blue, traditional style **Malabar Muslim Jama-Ath Mosque.** The prayer room is upstairs, and from the gallery you can look down on the quiet palm-shaded cemetery behind.

Turn right as you leave, go back down Victoria Street and you will pass Singapore's oldest **Muslim cemetery,** where the graves are arranged under the sweet smelling frangipani trees. Records as far

back as 1836 show that Malay princes were buried here.

Further down, on the opposite side of Victoria Street, are shops selling religious paraphernalia, like bright red and gold religious artefacts and altars, candles, and brass and jade statues. The Bugis MRT station is just ahead.

Typical Arab Sreet vendor

Lian Shan Shuang Lin Monastery

11. Town, Temple and a Revolutionary's Villa

Get right off the beaten track: meet Singaporeans in a housing estate; visit a Chinese temple in the neighbourhood; and gain an insight into Sun Yat Sen's activities in his former headquarters.

Prancing stone lion

Either take a taxi directly to **Lian Shan Shuang Lin Monastery** (formerly known as Siong Lim Temple), literally the **Twin Grove of the Lotus Mountain Buddhist Temple**, or ride in the cool comfort of the MRT on the North line to **Toa Payoh**. Exit from the MRT station for the bus terminus where numbers 8, 26, 31, 90 and 142 will bring you to the largest Buddhist temple in Singapore. Built in 1908, the temple's name commemorates Buddha's birth in a sacred wooded grove, and his death between two auspicious Bodhi trees.

Over a curved bridge is a decorated gateway to the temple courtyard. Enter the temple and wander around the spacious interior. Observe worshippers repeatedly bowing in prayer with incense sticks between their palms, asking the gods for good fortune and health, or sitting in silent meditation beneath the beautiful ceiling. The marble Buddhas from Thailand are impressive, as is the large golden laughing Buddha. The garden with its great rocks is peaceful, but is much smaller today than it was when the temple

Rolls of hell-money

was built, as half the land area was donated to the Housing and Development Board (HDB) years ago for low-cost housing. These flats are the type in which the majority of Singaporeans live today. Long external corridors lead to individual flats, which often reflect the race of the occupants; the Chinese display red banners or lanterns outside and Indians have pictures of their deities above the door. Today, as part of a government upgrading scheme, many of these older HDB housing estates are undergoing major refurbishments.

Cross the road and take the bus back to the interchange. Just across Lorong 6 Toa Payoh you'll see a small red and white tower in a park. **Toa Payoh Town Garden** is a peaceful oasis of ponds and willows, shady angsanas, bamboo and flowering trees. Created by the HDB in the early 1970s, it is a pleasant place to relax. Climb up the tower and take a look around.

At the other end of the park is a footbridge. As you cross it, you'll see a pale yellow colonial bungalow to the right, the **Sun Yat Sen Villa**. Typical of the early 20th century style, it blends Palladian with Chinese and Malay architecture, with wide verandas, high ceilings and the servants' quarters at the back. The caretaker speaks little English but will let you in free. Pick up a free booklet.

Originally named Bin Chan House, it became the headquarters of Dr Sun Yat Sen and his communist revolutionaries in the 1910s on his visits to Singapore. It was here that he finalised many plans for the overthrow of the Manchu dynasty in China. Dr Sun's life and exploits are traced in old photographs, letters and maps downstairs. Upstairs is a touching display of photos and possessions of those who endured life in Syonan-to, as Singapore was known the Japanese Occupation. From here retrace your steps to the garden and perhaps have supper by the lake. There are plenty of cheap restaurants and shops nearby, so take your time to explore the area.

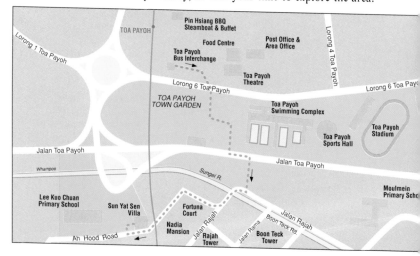

The Botanic Gardens, the perfect place to relax in on a hot afternoon

12. The Botanic Gardens

A pleasant stroll through soothing green; lush greenery, a vivid orchid garden and peaceful parkland.

Where Holland Road and Napier Road join, just 10 minutes' walk from Orchard Road, a white gateway leads into beautiful gardens, more than five times as old as the nation itself. The **Botanic Gardens**, which extend over 32ha (80 acres), contain over 3,000 species of trees and shrubs, in areas as varied as virgin jungle, marshland, lakes and formal gardens. It is here that the first rubber trees in Asia were grown, from which Henry Ridley started the rubber industry of Malaysia. Most trees in the garden are named, so you learn as you go along.

In the orchard you can see exactly how orchids are grown from seed. There are more than 2,500 plants with 250 different hybrids here, including Singapore's national flower, the purple *Vanda Miss Joaquim*. A riot of glorious colour, this spectacular garden is often crowded with wedding parties taking photographs. At dawn and in the evenings, you'll see health-conscious Singaporeans doing *tai-chi*, a graceful Chinese art, or joggers in their Reeboks sweating it out amid the greenery.

Pack a picnic lunch or perhaps a snack for the evening when it's cooler and sit back and relax un-

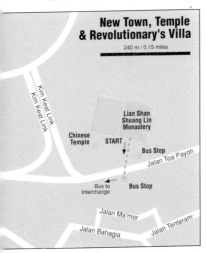

New Town, Temple & Revolutionary's Villa

240 m / 0.15 miles

Kim Keat Link
Kim Keat Link

Chinese Temple

START

Lian Shan Shuang Lin Monastery

Bus Stop

Jalan Toa Payoh

Bus to Interchange

Bus Stop

Jalan Ma'mor

Jalan Bahagia

Jalan Tenteram

Orchids galore

der the shade of the trees. Alternatively, cross the road to **Taman Serasi** food centre which is famous for its *Roti John* (the Asian version of French toast made with eggs and minced meat) and fresh soursop fruit juice.

13. Sentosa

An afternoon on Singapore's most organised offshore islands.

Whether your penchant is for history, nature or simply fun for the kids, Sentosa island offers a contrast to the frenetic city atmosphere of Singapore. A basic admission ticket gives you access to the island, its park areas and beaches plus unlimited rides on buses and the monorail. Most of the other attractions have their own admission charges.

There are several ways of getting there: across a causeway to Sentosa by bus or taxi or on foot; by ferry from the World Trade Centre; or by cable car from the cable car towers either at Mount Faber or the one next to the World Trade Center. Buy a one-way cable car ticket to **Sentosa** and enjoy the splendid view of the port and Keppel Shipyard. Sentosa was once known as 'Pulau Blakang Mati', roughly translates into 'Island of the Back of the Dead', as local pirates used to bury their victims here. Today, its macabre past is all forgotten as tourists and locals flock in increasing numbers to this popular leisure spot.

The ferry terminal on Sentosa Island

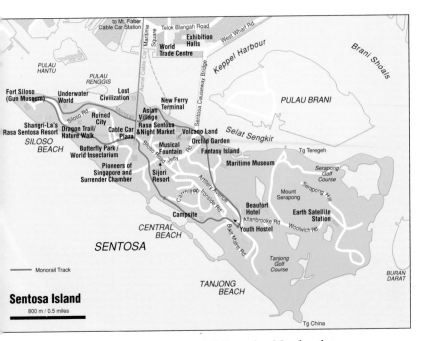

Sentosa Island

800 m / 0.5 miles

Get off the cable car and turn left from the ticket booth to your first stop, the **Images of Singapore** exhibition, where wax figures recount the history of Singapore from its earliest days to British colonial times. The adjoining **Surrender Chambers** takes you through the years of World War II with waxworks depicting the surrender of the British and the Japanese.

Butterfly and insect fiends will enjoy the pretty park just opposite. Otherwise, take the monorail to **Fort Siloso** to relive the fort's history from the 1800s to early 1940s. You can then continue your exploration of the island by bus or monorail, although cycling is a popular option. The list of attractions are many and highlights include: **Underwater World**, **Butterfly Park & Insect Kingdom Museum**, **Asian Village**, **Nature Walk** and **Sentosa Orchid Gardens** among others, and two beaches for swimming and recreation. **Fantasy Island's** 32 water rides and slides are guaranteed to send you into a tizzy but if you prefer something slightly more sedate, visit **Volcanoland**, a multimedia theme park that takes you into a subterranean journey into the earth.

The **Musical Fountain** display starts at half-hourly intervals from 4pm to 5.30pm daily. The night performances include light and laser effects (half-hourly at 7.30pm, 8.30pm and 9.30pm nightly).

If the island charms you enough, consider staying at any three of the luxury hotels on the island: the colonial-style **Beaufort** (tel: 275-0331) or **Sijori Resort** (tel: 275-0220) or the less expensive **Shangri-La's Rasa Sentosa Resort** (tel: 275-0100). There are restaurants at all three hotels but if you prefer something cheaper, try the food court called Rasa Sentosa.

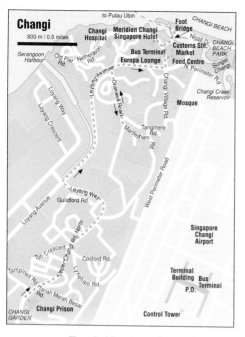

Changi

800 m / 0.5 miles

to Pulau Ubin

Serangoon Harbour
Old Pier Rd.
Netheravon Rd.
Loyang Avenue
Loyang Way
Loyang Crescent
Cranwell Road
Changi Hospital
Meridien Changi Singapore Hotel
Bus Terminal
Europa Lounge
Foot Bridge
CHANGI BEACH
Nicoll Dr.
CHANGI BEACH PARK
Customs Stn.
Market
Food Centre
N. Perimeter Rd.
Sungei Changi
Changi Village Rd.
Mosque
Changi Creek Reservoir
Tangmere Rd.
Martlesham Rd.
West Perimeter Road
Loyang Avenue
Leyang Way
Guildford Rd.
Singapore Changi Airport
Toh Crescent
Upper Changi Rd. North
Cosford Rd.
Lyneham Rd.
Terminal Building
Bus Terminal
P.O.
Tampines Rd.
Tanah Merah Besar Rd.
CHANGI GARDEN
Changi Prison
Control Tower

A trip to the east of the island in remembrance of prisoners of World War II. Visit the Changi Prison Chapel and Museum and then look at the famous Changi Murals. Afterwards, a stroll along the beach and perhaps a boat ride over to Pulau Ubin.

Take a taxi to **Changi Prison** (Monday to Saturday 9.30am– 4.30pm, closed on Sunday and public holiday), from the city centre. If you just want to visit the museum and chapel and then return, ask the driver to wait for you. A cheaper alternative is to take the MRT to **Tanah Merah** station and hop on bus no. 2.

The museum is just to the left of the main gate of the forbidding-looking edifice of the prison. The museum gives a moving insight

into life as a prisoner of war in Changi Prison, which housed as many as 3,000 prisoners at one time. WRM Haxworth's drawings and George Aspinall's photographs once seen is seldom forgotten, such is their impact. Nor will the suffering of the POWs. In the little **Prison Chapel**, cards expressing fond memories and gratitude are affixed to a board to the left of the altar, and you are invited to pick a flower from the garden and place it on the altar in remembrance of these brave men and women who suffered during the war. A service is held at the Chapel from 5.30 to 7 on Sunday evenings. There is also a little shop selling a selection of books on the war period, as well as souvenirs.

To visit the **Changi Murals** in Changi Airbase Camp (Monday to Saturday 10am–5pm), turn right out of the gate and drive straight on, pass the crossroads and straight on as it bends left as Loyang Way. Continue until you reach Loyang Avenue, where you make a right turn. Eventually you will find Cranwell Road on the right, which leads to Martlesham Road where, at the Guardroom of Block 122, ask for the key to St Luke's Chapel where the murals are found. At Block 151, despite difficulties in acquiring materials,

Stanley Warren painted five beautiful murals depicting scenes from the life of Christ.

After the war, the murals, covered with paint, were almost forgotten, but interest was later aroused. Warren was finally located in London and persuaded to return to Singapore to restore them in 1963, and again in 1982 to do further work. Today, the chapel is once again a place of worship and a tribute to men's faith under duress.

Once you're done, turn right out of Cranwell Road and then take Changi Village Road to the left. On the corner is **George Photo**, where George Aspinall learned how to develop photographs. Taking the bend to the left, you will come to the **Changi Meridien Hotel**, a popular hotel for travellers in transit because of its proximity to Changi Airport. Here, you might like to have a drink, and visit the

Changi Beach

exhibition on the 5th floor where more reproductions of George Aspinall's photographs and details of the murals and information on World War II are displayed.

To explore this end of the island, retrace your steps to George Photo where you turn left to the bus terminal and car park. Cross the little bridge and take the footpath to **Changi Beach**, deserted mainly during the week, but packed at weekends. It's a lovely place to wander at leisure, away from the bustle of the city, watching the ships sailing to and from the port.

If you feel like a boat trip, make your way back over the bridge and down to the **Changi Jetty** on your right. There are always plenty of boatmen ready to go to **Pulau Ubin**, the island you saw over to the left from the beach. Usually you wait for 12 passengers and pay S$1.50 each to get there, but you can make up the difference and bargain. Getting back costs the same.

Over on Pulau Ubin, take a ride on one of the island's rickety taxis to see the island which is still rustic, although soon to be developed. During the weekends, Pulau Ubin is a favourite haunt for mountain-biking enthusiasts from Singapore. Walk or cycle around the village (there is a bicycle rental shop near the jetty), and if you like, have supper at the seafood restaurant near the jetty.

Back in Singapore, you might like to enjoy 'Happy Hour', at the **Europa Lounge and Restaurant** at the corner of Changi Village Road, and then perhaps some local fare at the food centre in Changi Village. To return, take a taxi or bus no. 2 back to the city. Otherwise, drive along the East Coast Parkway (ECP) on your way back to the city centre, stopping to eat at any of the innumerable restaurants serving delicious seafood (see Itinerary 22 *Pick & Mix*).

15. Oriental Gardens and Tang Dynasty City

Two distinctly different gardens and a visit back into time at Tang Dynasty City

Take the MRT to the Chinese Garden station for a ride which takes you above ground for much of the way out to Jurong, in the west of the island.

The **Chinese Garden** or Yu-Hua Yuen (open daily 9am–7pm) in Yuan Ching Road is modelled after the Imperial Sung Dynasty style of the Summer Palace in Beijing. Here, bridges and archways harmonise with nature, and the exotic lakeside pagodas offer a glo-

Japanese Gardens

Charming water courtyard at the Chinese Garden

rious view of the gardens. Walk along the banks of the lake, wander around the interesting Herb Garden and the cheery Ixora Garden, and inhale the scents in the Garden of Fragrance. A top attraction here is the Garden of Beauty or Yun Xiu Yuan, a Suzhou-style garden with some 3,000 miniature bonsai trees.

Then, take the 65-m (214-ft) long bridge over to the **Japanese Garden** (open daily 9am–7pm). Also called 'The Garden of Tranquillity', it is a statement of stark simplicity, the small shrubs, stone lanterns and miniature waterfall all conspiring to induce a

feeling of calm and serenity. These two gardens show different Asian approaches to horticulture and nature, and give an insight into the distinct Chinese and Japanese cultures.

Another dose of Chinese history can be had at the nearby **Tang Dynasty City** at 2 Yuan Ching Road (open daily 10.30am–6pm, tel: 261-1116), a recreation of the ancient capital of Chang An during China's Tang Dynasty period (AD618–907).

Welcome to the Tang Dynasty

Spread over 12ha (30 acres), visitors can experience what life must have been like during this period of Chinese history. Imposing grey brick walls with strategically placed guard towers enclose the city. Inside, there are replicas of the Great Wall of China, Chinese terracotta warriors, pagodas, a traditional Chinese tea shop, and other recreations of the Tang Dynasty era. In addition, various shows like pugilistic displays, traditional craft work and wedding processions are staged throughout the day.

Evening splendour at the Raffles Hotel

Evening Itineraries

16. Raffles Revisited

Ascend 70 storeys for high tea and a bird's eye view over Singapore, then adjourn to Raffles Hotel for a romantic evening.

For a heart-stopping view of Singapore and beyond, take the MRT to City Hall station. As you emerge from City Hall, take the exit for the Westin Stamford Hotel and make your way to the special lift to the **Compass Rose** (tel: 338-8585). It will whisk you up 70 storeys for a breathtaking view. Indulge in either high tea, from 11.30am to 5.30pm or if you're there a little later, enjoy a sundowner, looking right across Singapore to Malaysia. The sun sets around 7pm, so it's well worth timing your refreshment till then. Take a look down at the peaceful courtyards and ornate buildings of the **Raffles Hotel** (tel: 337-1886), and then make your way to **Beach Road** where 'The Grand Old Lady of the East' presides.

Follow Rudyard Kipling's advice and 'Feed at Raffles when visiting Singapore'. Restored to its 1920s chic, the Raffles has not lost its magic and is still the most romantic place to dine in Singapore. Turn into the courtyard, and ahead you'll see the elegant facade bathed in yellow light. Ascend the steps and step back into a bygone era. Wander through the lobby and perhaps enjoy a Singapore Sling at the **Long Bar**. Dining options are numerous, from the upscale **Raffles Grill**, fusion cuisine at **Doc Cheng's**, the **Tiffin Room**, with its spicy curries, or the **Bar and Billiard Room** where you'll find the very billiard table under which the last tiger in Singapore is said to have been shot. Later, check out the hotel's fascinating past at the **museum** (open daily 10am–9pm). Next door is **Jubilee Hall Theatre**, a venue for drama and other theatrical events. Somerset Maugham summed up the spirit of the hotel best when he said that 'Raffles stands for all the fables of the exotic East'.

Savour local cuisine under the stars at a hawker centre.

No visit to Singapore would be complete without a visit to the hawker stalls, and some of the best are to be found at **Newton Circus**. So dress in cool, casual clothes, take the MRT to Newton station and make your way to the open-air food centre across.

Take your time and just wander around first. There are over 80 stalls here and the choice of food and drink is mind-boggling: Chinese, Indian and Malay. There is fresh seafood — fish, cockles, mussels, oysters (usually priced by the 100g) — usually barbecued and served with hot and spicy *sambal* sauce and *satay* sticks of marinated beef, chicken or mutton. Then there's Malay *nasi padang* (about S$4 for rice with your choice of side dishes), noodles of all shapes, sizes and flavours, Chinese fish porridge, Malay *nasi goreng* (fried rice), Indian *murtabak* (savoury pancake); you name it, it's definitely here somewhere.

Lobsters galore

Newton is always buzzing with action — Indian men whirling pieces of dough and Chinese women tossing noodles, steaming pots and bubbling woks, and harried women bearing plates of steaming food. If the rough and tumble of open-air hawker centres (another good bet is **Lau Pa Sat** in the Central Business District) do not appeal, check out the air-conditioned food courts in shopping malls instead. The food here is usually more expensive by a dollar or two to offset the higher rents and air-conditioning. **Picnic** at Scotts shopping centre, in Scotts Road, is a pioneer of the concept but try also **Kopi Tiam** chain of food courts: the latest one opened on the Orchard strip at the basement of Hotel Le Meridien. Other worthwhile food courts are found at the basements of Orchard Cineleisure, Ngee Ann City, Tanglin and Suntec shopping malls. Most are open daily 10.30am to 10pm.

Eating out – Singapore style

Whether you dine in hawker centres like Newton or food courts, the etiquette is always the same: get someone in your party to sit at an empty table to reserve it while the others walk around to choose their food. Make your orders at the stall and tell the stallholder your table number, although in food courts self-service is the norm. In hawker centres like Newton you only pay when the food comes and do remember the cardinal rule – no tipping.

18. Harbour Cruises

Cruise in style and enjoy the glittering night scene of Singapore from offshore.

While there are cruises all day long, there is nothing quite like watching the sunset as you float past Singapore's coast and offshore islands on an old Chinese-style junk. As the sun sets at about 7pm, the best option is Fairwind's Starlite Dinner Cruise which sets sail from Clifford Pier at 6pm. You'll have more than enough time to savour the sights and the full buffet spread of Singaporean food on this 2ᵛ-hour cruise. For bookings, call Fairwind Harbour Cruises at tel: 533-3432. Watertours (tel: 533-9811) also operates a similar dinner cruise, called Twilight Cruise, on a Chinese junk. Clifford Pier, in the heart of old Singapore, is where the Chinese junks are usually berthed.

If you are at the Raffles' Landing Site near Boat Quay or at Clarke Quay, you can take a short 30-minute river cruise on a bumboat down the Singapore River and learn something about the pivotal role the river has played in Singapore's development. Boats leave at regular intervals between 9am and 11pm daily (tel: 339-6833).

Romantic sunset harbour cruise

Go back in time to the good old days of the 1920s and dine in an elegant mansion overlooking the Straits of Singapore.

Take a taxi to the **Alkaff Mansion**, up on Telok Blangah Hill Park, in time to enjoy sundowners out on the terrace. There, relaxing in the lush tropical gardens, you can take in the view of the harbour and skyline of Singapore.

When the sun has set, go inside for dinner. You'll feel as if you are the guest in a spacious private house. The high ceilings with silent fans make the interior pleasantly cool. Softly-lit lamps, original prints, rugs on the polished floor, and antique furniture from the 1920s enhance the atmosphere so reminiscent of the early years of Singapore life. This is the Singapore of Somerset Maugham and novels like *Tanamera*.

Gracious dining

In the hall downstairs is a curry buffet spread, while upstairs you can choose from an *a la carte* continental menu or better still, the Rijstaffel – a traditional Indonesian meal comprising 15 delicately spiced dishes. A procession of graceful women in *sarong kebayas* will bring the dishes to you, a feast for the eyes as well as the palate. Just sit back and enjoy the live music, the relaxed, romantic atmosphere and the gentle, attentive service.

On Friday and Saturday nights, the Alkaff Mansion sets out a barbecue on the terrace so that guests can enjoy the balmy tropical night while dining alfresco. The only trouble is that it gets too balmy for most people. Tip: the air-conditioned restrooms are pleasant escape when the heat gets too stifling for you. No reservations are taken for the barbecue, so make your way up the hill early and enjoy a leisurely drink before dinner.

After dinner, sip your nightcap in the verandah bar, or outside under the stars. For reservations, call 278-6979.

Old-world charm at the Alkaff

Pub crawling and people watching on Orchard Road.

So who says you can't have a good time in Singapore? The city isn't Bangkok, or the risque port it once used to be, but you can go pub crawling, drink yourself under the table and still pick up a companion or two in the process. Be prepared to pay highly for your drinks because of heavy import taxes: unless you drink during the discounted 'Happy Hour' (or hours as the case usually is), pub crawling is definitely going to burn a big hole in your pocket. Which is why most Singaporeans prefer to eat instead! Many hotels have discos and bars, and karaoke lounges are aplenty. Here are some suggestions for an evening's revelry in Orchard Road, although there are numerous watering holes in other parts of the city.

This is going to be one long night so start with supper at the tail end of Orchard Road at **Dan Ryan's Chicago Grill** (next to the Regent hotel) where the atmosphere is laid-back and the portions American-sized – a great way to start the evening. Then walk down to Orchard hotel where you'll probably hear the sounds of guitars and singing from its aptly named **Sidewalk Cafe**. In the hotel's shopping arcade there is **Muddy Murphy's Irish Pub** where Irish bands entertain nightly and the friendly expat crowds are a little raucous. **Heaven**, at neighbouring Orchard Parade hotel, attracts a snooty clientele of mainly models and flight crew. R&B is the music of play here.

Just behind the hotel, on the corner of Cuscaden Road, is a vintage car bursting from the wall above the entrance to the **Hard Rock Cafe**. You'll be assured of a lively welcome here, even if – like all Hard Rock cafes everywhere – you have to wait a while to get in, especially on weekends. When you get a table eventually, things will move fast. The deejay spins mainly retro here (yes, they're calling music of the 80s retro these days!).

Just across the road, at Orchard Towers on level 4 is a former cinema turned nightspot with a reputation of being a pick-up joint, the cavernous **Top Ten**. The local and international bands are good, and there's plenty of bar and dancing space, while the tiered seating makes people-watching easy. At the junction of Orchard and Scotts roads on the left is the swanky **Venom** at the Pacific Plaza. It attracts the young and flashy as DJs spin music to the techno beat.

If you aren't suitably inebriated by now, head further down Orchard Road to the sprawling **Sparks** entertainment complex. Its huge dance floor occupying the 8th floor of Ngee Ann City is the curent 'happening' place for would-be wannabes. Then there is the sleek **Lava Lounge** with its kitschy decor proclaiming (no, make that shouting) a style of its own at Orchard Building. Lava is one of Singapore's hippest clubs with a disco and karaoke rooms to add to its appeal. Next door at the Specialists' Shopping Centre is award-winning nightspot **Pleasure Dome**. The disco plays mainstream retro fare.

21. Boat and Clarke Quays

Trendy restaurants, music and karaoke bars – nightlife with a Singapore flavour.

New York has Soho, Hong Kong the Lan Kwai Fong district, and Singapore, well ... um... er. For years, nothing really until the emergence of **Boat Quay** in the late 1980s. For such a place to develop and thrive, ambience is everything, and everything was done to create the right atmosphere for Boat Quay. After the authorities cleaned up the Singapore River in 1985, the defunct warehouses along its banks were re-zoned for retail outlets, restaurants and bars. Owners were required to preserve the traditional facades of the shophouses and maintain the general ambience. Today, the ever-bustling strip is home to over 50 bars and restaurants.

Boat Quay is set against the background of the Central Business District's (CBD) skyscrapers. The riverside promenade is lined with trendy watering holes, karaoke lounges, eastern and western and everything in-between type of restaurants. This is the favourite haunt of the banking crowds, yuppies and tourists as well as Singaporeans who love the nightlife. They flock to the 300-m (984-ft) stretch which alternates between quiet spots of riverside dining and loud music bars.

Boat Quay begins with **Pasta Fresca Da Salvatore** (one of several outlets serving decent pastas and pizzas on the island). There's a string of trendy but expensive pubs, bars, karaoke lounges (beer prices average about S$18 per jug). Bar flies can pick from several watering holes, including **Harry's Quayside** (where the infamous Barings trader Nick Leeson lived it up and allegedly dropped his pants for a spot of mooning) and **Culture Club**. Some

Boat Quay buzzes by night

recommended restaurant stops include **Sukhothai** (Thai); **Kinara** (Northern Indian) and **Izumi** (Japanese). Near the other end of the quay is **Superbowl** (Chinese congee and noodles). **Tower** bookstore is next to a **Coffee Bean & Tea Leaf** shop which is just before Elgin Bridge. If you don't want to pub crawl you can always do some late night browsing (Tower opens from 11am to midnight) and read with a *latte* in hand by the river.

Behind Boat Quay is **Circular Road** where the restaurants and bars don't charge as much and where there is a real taste of post-war Singapore. It has the feel of a back street with its numerous trading and textile stores. Cosmopolitan pubs (like the distinctly British **Molly Malone's**) and restaurants (**Moomba** serving *haute* Australian cuisine) sit side-by-side small companies set up in shophouses.

Cross Elgin Bridge and walk up river to **Clarke Quay** which bills itself as a Festival Village and does come across as a family sort of place. The waterside here is as lively as Boat Quay after sunset with over 20 restaurants and pubs. There is shopping here with over 100 shops in the converted godowns, and push-cart vendors. It's now

Clarke Quay shop front

also the home of the famous **Satay Club** stalls (previously from the Esplanade) and an air-conditioned **Hawker's Alley**. Four pedestrian lanes radiate out from the centre of the village where the **Gazebo** outdoor beer pub is. Live bands perform here nightly. On Wednesday and Friday nights, there is a traditional Chinese opera performance (7.45–8.30pm) by a local cultural troupe. You can also

80

visit a picture gallery that traces the 100-year history of the Singapore River on the 2nd floor of Merchant Court building.

The retail shops offer a variety of merchandise ranging from fashion and accessories, gifts and souvenirs, antiques, curios, home furnishings, watches and jewellery. The **Clarke Quay Adventure Ride** is a Disney-inspired ride which takes visitors on a boat ride past sound and light displays tracing the history of Singapore from a pirates' lair to the end of colonial rule in 1945.

22. Chilli Crabs at East Coast

Less a meal, more an experience. Crabs drenched in hot chilli gravy to be bashed with a hammer and prised open with fingers.

Dress very casually (the gravy gets everywhere so don't wear white). Take a taxi and tell the driver to take you to the **UDMC Seafood Centre** at the East Coast. The makeshift seafood establishments of 20 years ago with sand underfoot and swaying palm trees has given way to a rash of seafood restaurants housed in three blocks of spanking-clean terraced restaurants.

Some seven seafood restaurants make up the centre and the crowds come thick and fast every night to chow down on chilli crabs, swallow squirming drunken prawns and crunch on crispy baby squids. Carloads of young Singaporeans, Japanese men clutching bottles of XO brandy and bewildered Caucasians add colour to an otherwise sterile environment of plastic chairs, formica-topped tables and strings of twinkling coloured bulbs.

Pick a restaurant, any one, as practically the same food is dished out everywhere (al-

Feast on seafood

though some swear that **Red House** is a notch above the others) and order. One medium Sri Lankan crab is sufficient for two people and will cost about S$25. When you've finished devouring all the flesh, ask for chunks of French loaf to be dipped into the piquant gravy and savoured.

You can also ask for the crabs to be grilled with black pepper. But be forewarned; keep a glass of water at hand. Other dishes to try are crispy fried baby squid, stuffed *you tiao* (dough sticks) and deep fried *soon hock* (snakehead fish). Ice-cold local Tiger or Anchor beer is the best drink to wash down this quintessential Singaporean meal.

EXCURSIONS

23. Johor Bahru

A glimpse of Malaysia and its relaxed pace of life.

Get away from the bustle of Singapore and explore **Johor Bahru**, the southernmost city in Peninsular Malaysia. The city is the capital of the State of Johor, one of 13 states which, along with Sabah and Sarawak in Borneo, form the Federation of Malaysia.

There are several ways of getting to this neighbouring state. If you hire a car from Singapore (Hertz, tel: 734-4646), make sure that your petrol tank is at least three-quarters full before leaving. Otherwise, you could be slapped with a fine of S$500. Petrol is cheaper in Malaysia, and this rule was introduced to prevent a loss of tax revenue in Singapore. There are two routes to Malaysia. The route via the Tuas Causeway is less prone to traffic jams but there is a 35-km (21¾ miles) detour to get to Johor Bahru once you get across the causeway. Go via the Woodlands Causeway instead, taking the Pan Island Expressway (PIE) and then the Bukit Timah Expressway (BKE). If you prefer a more scenic route, drive via

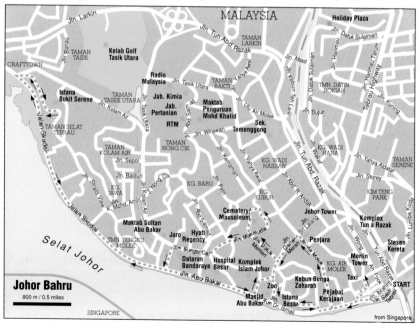

Johor Bahru
800 m / 0.5 miles

Bukit Timah Road. If you do, make a stop at the **Kranji War Cemetery and Singapore State Cemetery**, a moving tribute to those who gave their lives in World War II in Southeast Asia.

Then drive across the 1.2-km (8-mile) causeway spanning the calm waters of the Straits of Johor to Malaysia. This road and rail link was completed in 1924 at a cost of 12 million Straits Dollars, and as you'll see from the long lines of lorries, it is vital for trade between Malaysia and Singapore. On the right of the causeway are enormous pipes which carry water from Johor to Singapore.

If you decide not to drive, call 296-7054/292-0198 for the Singapore-Johor Taxi Service and ask to be picked up from your hotel for the drive to Johor Bahru (Singapore taxis are not permitted to drive into Johor).

Another alternative is to take the Singapore-Johor Express bus which leaves Ban San Street, behind Rochor Centre, for the Johor Bus Station. Otherwise, SBS bus no. 170 can travel to Johor Bahru from Queen Street Terminal in just 30 minutes, although, with frequent stops along the way and traffic jams during peak hours, the journey may take longer. Once in Johor, you can arrange for a taxi for four or five hours at about M$20 an hour. Whatever mode of transport you choose, don't forget your passport.

All visitors must fill in immigration and currency declaration forms before entering Malaysia. In addition, those driving in must purchase a toll coupon of S$1 from any petrol station in Singapore and pay RM (Ringgit Malaysia) 2.10 at the Malaysian side of the causeway. The exchange rate is about RM2.30 to S$1, so make sure that you change enough money (but not more than RM1,000 as stipulated by recent currency restrictions) before you enter the country. But don't fret if you don't: there are money changers in Johor Bahru.

Malaysia is a parliamentary democracy, but there are still nine Sultans who, although bereft of political power, remain

School children at Kranji War Memorial and Cemetery

The stately court house

influential as landowners and heads of religion in their states. They take turns to be King of Malaysia for a five-year period. The present Sultan Iskandar of Johor was king from 1984 to 1989, and the history of his family is part of the fascination of Johor.

Just past the white columns of the court house, you'll see an elegant white building with a blue roof, the **Istana Besar** or Grand Palace (open daily except Friday 10am–5pm). At the traffic lights turn right up **Jalan Air Molek** into the grounds of what was until 1936 the residence of the sultans of Johor. Overlooking the Straits of Johor, this lovely palace is now a museum. You may hire a guide at the museum (or call ahead and arrange for one, tel: (607) 388-5033, at RM60 for two hours).

Start in the Dewan or hall, where the history of the state is traced from the earliest days of the Johor-Riau-Lingga-Pahang Empire to the present. Then, walk into the palace proper and enjoy the feel of the luxurious carpets as you wander about the throne room and the family bedrooms. The furnishings are stupendous, and include a Baccarat crystal dining table and chairs, elaborately-carved Indian furniture, enormous four-poster beds and sparkling chandeliers. Finally, you enter the splendid banqueting hall, ready for a sumptuous feast. It is decked out in the Johor royal colour, yellow, and the British royal colour, blue. Ties with Britain are evident in the many gifts and honours bestowed in the past, as well as in the family tree. In fact, in 1935 a Scottish girl became sultana.

The friendship between the Johor Sultan and Emperor Hirohito, which preserved Johor from destruction during World War II, is

evident in the fascinating gifts from Japan, and the replica of a Japanese teahouse in the garden.

There are galleries displaying magnificent collections of silver and gold, traditional Malay costumes, betel nut sets intricately fashioned in silver, and a room with many different kinds of *keris* (a traditional Malay dagger with an undulating blade). In the Hunting Gallery are trophies won at horse racing and hunting fests. The latter include stag heads, numerous ivory tusks and a huge tiger.

Take your time to enjoy the fascinating insight into Johor's past and present. Before you leave, explore the Japanese garden by the traditional teahouse (not open for tea these days, unfortunately). Otherwise, take the path down to the right of the exit, to the craft shop and small refreshment bar at the back, where you'll find the most delicious *nasi lemak* (coconut flavoured rice served with a variety of condiments). Opposite is the **Johore Tourist Information Centre (JOTIC)** (tel: (607) 224-2000).

Return to Jalan Air Molek and turn left at the first traffic junction, and left again into Jalan Gertak Merah until you see the ornate Masjid Abu Bakar on your right. Turn right and follow the beach-side road. Carry on for a kilometre or so until you see a great Japanese-style palace high on your right.

At the sign for **Istana Bukit Serene**, turn right and almost immediately left in front of the Kebun Bunga Istana, or palace nursery, to the corner of Jalan Tahar to **Craft town**. Here you can visit a *batik* factory and watch delicate flowers being hand-drawn in beeswax using a *chanting*, a metal holder with a spout. The process is fascinating to watch; a selection of handicrafts are sold in the adjoining shop for those sufficiently mesmerised by the art of *batik*.

Go back and up the hill to admire the view from the top outside the Istana Bukit Serene, the present home of the Sultan of Johor. You'll probably be ready for lunch now, so drive back along Jalan Skudai until you see a sign for **Marina Seafood Villa** on your left. Turn in and enjoy the rustic atmosphere, glorious views and excellent food.

After lunch, drive on down Jalan Abu Bakar and turn left just before you reach the mosque, **Masjid Abu Bakar**. Walk around the ground. Unfortunately, tourists in the past have not respected the sanctity of the place, which is why non-Muslims are no longer allowed inside. The building is beautiful, even from the outside and there's plenty of life, with vendors hawking prayer mats and paintings.

Leave by the green arch on the other side; bear left up the hill on Jalan Gertak Merah

and then left into Jalan Datuk Menteri where you will come to the **Muslim Cemetery and Mausoleum**. The latter is usually closed, but you can drive up to the yellow building for a look at the graves. All point to Mecca, and the stones, one at the head and one at the foot of the uncremated body, indicate by their shape whether a man or woman lies there. The round stones are for men, and the flat ones for the women.

On leaving, turn left and then left again into Jalan Mahmudiah and then right down Jalan Cik Besar Zubaidah. You're in a Malay *kampong* or village now. The houses are invariably on stilts and surrounded by flowering plants and fruit trees. It's a relaxed lifestyle, and at 6B, ask the owner, Ungku Adleen Ungku Abu Bakar, if you can visit her home. Take your shoes off and look around and remember to leave a small token of your appreciation.

Then, retrace your steps up along Jalan Mahmudiah, turn right past the whole of the cemetery and follow the road as it turns right. On your left is **Dataran Bandaraya**, which commemorates Johor Bahru's status as a city, and on the next corner is a sign for 'JARO' where you turn right to the **Johor Area Rehabilitation Organisation**. Handicrafts made by the physically handicapped are sold here. Go downstairs and watch books being bound in fine leather and baskets of all shapes and sizes being made.

After that it's time to return to the hurly burly of Singapore, having taken a glimpse of a slower, calmer side of Asia.

Singapore from the opposite shore

Journey to Bangkok on a luxurious train.

The legendary romance of the *Orient Express*, now transplanted in the exotic Far East, recreates one of the world's great railway journeys. Even more luxurious than the original *Venice Simplon-Orient-Express* train in Europe, the *Eastern and Orient Express* offers a fascinating overland trip to or from Singapore, a chance to appreciate the lush countryside which others merely fly over, and to enjoy the romance of travel while being pampered by attentive staff.

From the comfortable compartments for two, with ensuite shower room, to the cosy ambience of the bar and the thrill of the open observation car, this train is like no other. Intricate carvings, gleaming brass fittings, luxurious fabrics and soft carpets create an atmosphere of elegance. Sit back and enjoy the passing scenery. Clusters of *kampong* houses framed by palm fronds and bougainvillea, lines of rubber trees interspersed with spiky oil palms and padi fields stretching out to distant blue hills rush pass in an ever-moving tableau as the train snakes its way through Malaysia and Thailand.

You simply watch the world go by, with no stifling heat, no exasperating traffic and no immigration hassles to bother you. The day is pleasantly relaxed, with delectable meals to look forward to and cocktails in the bar and lounge cars. Breakfast and afternoon tea are served in your compartment while lunch and dinner are more fastidious occasions in the cosy ambience of the dining cars. Remember to pack some semi-formal wear for dinner if you don't wish to look too out of place in these luxurious surroundings.

A feast for the senses

Passengers can stretch their legs and marvel at the illuminated minarets and domes of the exotic railway station in Kuala Lumpur. In Penang, an excursion on the ferry offers a chance to explore the temples and shops of Georgetown. The journey between Bangkok and Singapore takes two nights, with shorter excursions to River Kwai from Bangkok or to Malacca from Singapore also available.

Prices for the Singapore–Bangkok leg, which includes all meals on board, begin at US$1,300 per person. For reservations call tel: 392-3500 in Singapore; tel: (171) 805-5100 in UK; tel: (800) 524-2420 in USA; and tel: 1-800-331-429 toll free in Australia.

25. Batam and Bintan

A few days of sun, sand and sea in the Riau islands.

For years, Singaporeans have grumbled about the absence of white sandy beaches on their island, the artificially created beaches of Sentosa notwithstanding. Now they have reason to complain no more. Within sight of Singapore, but almost worlds away, are the two Indonesian islands of **Batam** and **Bintan**. They are part of 3,000 islands belonging to the Riau Archipelago and present a very different experience from ritzy Singapore. A few days lazing by the beach resorts of one or the other, or both, is the perfect antidote when the buzz of Singapore proves too heady. In fact, quite a number of Singaporeans make Batam and Bintan their weekend getaway (making it a good reason to go on a weekday instead), thanks in part to the convenient high-speed catamaran services between Singapore and these islands.

Batam is some 20km (13 miles) south of Singapore and is the closer of the two islands. About two-thirds the size of Singapore, Batam is an important industrial centre, thanks to oil, minerals and forestry. In recent years it has also turned to the tourist market, attracting Singaporeans with its golf courses, beaches, duty-free shopping and cheap seafood. Regular ferry services ply between the **World Trade Centre** and the **Tanah Merah Ferry Terminal** (TMFT) in Singapore to **Sekupang** and **Nongsa** ferry points in Batam respectively. The journey itself lasts only half an hour, but immigration and waiting time, plus transfer to a hotel in total takes about an hour longer.

Cottages at Turi Beach Resort

Skip the town of Nagoya, the island's largest, which was built by Japanese soldiers during World War II but bears little resemblance to its Japanese namesake, and head instead for the beaches. One of the loveliest is **Nongsa** beach where the **Turi Beach Resort** takes pride of place. A cluster of Balinese-styled cottages nestled on a hillside sloping to the sea, the resort is the perfect getaway. Call the Singapore office at 273-5055 for hotel and ferry bookings.

Above-water dining at the Kelong restaurant, Sol Elite Bintan

Bintan, nearly three times the size of Singapore at 1,030 sq km (398 sq miles) presents an even more attractive option. Pulau Bintan or 'Star Island' is the largest island in the Riau chain. Most of the island is made up of thick jungle, swamp and mountains with isolated pockets of people living in villages. But like Batam, development is catching on fast. Almost the entire northern shore, with its dazzling powder-white beaches, has been developed into a mega tourist area called Bintan Resorts by a Singapore business conglomerate. The pristine white sand beaches and clear aquamarine waters of this area has attracted even the likes of Club Med to join the other five major resorts here.

Getting to Bintan is a cinch: a high-speed catamaran zips you over in 45 minutes from Singapore's TMFT to Bintan's Bandar Bentan Telani ferry terminal, conveniently located near the north shore resorts. Whether you choose to stay in a private jacuzzi villa at the upscale **Banyan Tree Bintan** (tel: 65-462-4800), experience **Club Med Ria Bintan** (tel: 65-738-4222) with its French-style beach culture, spend a few nights at the stylish **Sol Elite Bintan** (tel: 62-334-3332) where the accent is on family fun or the laid-back chalet-style **Sol Mayang Sari Beach Resort** (65-732-8515), or

Sol Elite Bintan by night

tee off at the 18-hole Jack Nicklaus and Ian Baker-Finch designed golf courses of the **Hotel Sedona Bintan Lagoon** (tel: 65-223-3223), almost everyone concurs on the 3 'R's of Bintan: rest, relax and rejuvenate.

Eating Out

Wherever you go in Singapore, you can be sure of finding something to eat, and it's invariably delicious. Eating is the national pastime, and from hawker stall to plush hotel, from fusion cuisine to exotic Thai dishes, the range is mind-boggling. Singapore's ethnic mix and the people's love of good food ensures that Chinese, Malay and Indian food is readily available.

In Singapore, you never simply refer to Chinese food. There are as many as 80 different styles of cooking, although in general people tend to think in terms of four or five main regions of China. Stir-frying is essentially Cantonese, perhaps the cuisine best known in the west. Freshness of ingredients is of paramount importance, and the flavouring is subtle. Not so often available elsewhere is the array of small delicacies served from bamboo baskets called *dim sum*. Hainanese chicken rice is a perennial favourite of locals – succulent chicken meat slices served with rice cooked in the stock, soup and three sauces: dark soya sauce, chilli, and ground ginger and garlic.

The delicate flavour and careful cooking of the Teochews, in particular their preference for clear soups, will appeal to purists. And for a long-lasting, sociable meal try steamboat, where you cook your own seafood, meat and vegetables in a pot of boiling broth. Taiwanese porridge, Hakka stuffed bean curd dishes, Hokkien fried

Indulge in fine dining

mee and *popiah* or spring rolls are favourites from other regions. If you love spicy food, the sensational Szechuan cuisine is beyond comparison. Prawns with dried chilli and the hot and sour soup are less a taste sensation and more like a gourmet experience.

The blending of pungent spices is the hallmark of Indian food and there is a wide range, from mild *tandoori* dishes to mind-blowing

Hot stuff at the Satay Club

spicy *vindaloo* curries. The Moghul influence is evident in the northern use of the clay oven. Wheat replaces rice as the staple, in the form of oven-baked *naan*. Little India abounds with restaurants of all regional foods.

The most famous of Malay delicacies is *satay*, pieces of marinated meat on bamboo sticks barbecued and served with peanut sauce and *ketupat* or compressed rice. Like much Malay food, the dish probably originated in Indonesia. Robustly spiced, these two cuisines have much in common.

Nasi padang is a choice of spiced dishes served with rice, *gado-gado* is a salad of steamed or raw vegetables, fried beancurd and potatoes with peanut sauce and garnished with *belinjau* nut chips. Other favourites include *nasi goreng* (fried rice), *soto ayam* (chicken broth with bean sprouts) and beef *rendang* (spicy beef).

But what of Singapore itself? The nearest thing to indigenous cuisine is a mix of Chinese, Malay and Indonesian influences as developed by the Straits-born Chinese, or Peranakan cuisine. *Popiah* (spring rolls) and *laksa lemak* (noodles in a coconut gravy), given the distinctive taste of *blacan* – shrimp paste – are some of the delicious results of this combination.

The nutman

91

Claypot speciality

The waters around Singapore ensure fresh supplies of seafood and excellent local fish such as *ikan merah* (red snapper) and pomfret. Seafood restaurants are abundant and one of Singapore's all-time favourite, and perhaps even the national dish is chilli crab (see Itinerary 22 *Pick & Mix*). Another contender for the national dish title is the hot and spicy fish head curry, originally Indian and now often cooked in Chinese or Malay variations.

What to Drink

All this food needs something to wash it down with, and the locally-brewed Tiger and Anchor beers are excellent accompaniment to Asian food. At Chinese banquets cognac is often the drink of choice, or Chinese tea, which you can have unlimited servings of. Wines and spirits of all kinds are usually available, with longer lists at restaurants serving western cuisine. And of course, you shouldn't leave Singapore without trying a Singapore Sling, a blend of gin, cherry brandy, Cointreau, pineapple juice and fresh lime.

Where to Go

Besides numerous restaurants, there are many food centres, some outdoor, some in air-conditioned shopping centres, where the hawkers produce delicious food at low, low prices. You can try all kinds of food, and watch it being cooked. Just place your order and indicate where you are sitting, and the food will be brought to you. There's no better way to sample a wide variety of local dishes at one

go. The most famous is **Newton Circus** (see Itinerary 17 *Pick & Mix*) and **Lau Pa Sat.**

In the following pages, a 3-course meal for two without drinks is categorised as follows:
Expensive = S$80 and above
Moderate = S$50–S$80
Inexpensive = S$50 and below

Entrance to the Nonya and Baba Restaurant

Cantonese

HAI TIEN LO CANTONESE RESTAURANT
The Pan Pacific Hotel
Tel: 336-8111
Extensive menu and excellent views. *Expensive*

NOBLE HOUSE
UIC Building
Tel: 227-0933
Delectable Cantonese cuisine in an elegant setting reminiscent of a palace courtyard. *Moderate*

SHANG PALACE RESTAURANT
Shangri-La Hotel
Tel: 730-2372
Excellent *dim sum* at lunchtime and a wide range of *a la carte* choices in the evening. *Expensive*

WAH LOK RESTAURANT
Carlton Hotel
Tel: 330-3588
One of the best Hong Kong restaurants in Singapore. *Dim sum* is very popular here, as are the *a la carte* dishes. *Moderate*

LEI GARDEN RESTAURANT
CHIJMES, Victoria Street
Tel: 339-7663
Highly recommended, especially for Peking duck and lobster. *Moderate*

MITZI CANTONESE RESTAURANT
24/26 Murray Street
Tel: 222-8281
Recommended by discerning locals. *Inexpensive*

Szechuan

DRAGON CITY
Novotel Orchid Inn
Tel: 254-5477
So good that you have to make reservations. *Expensive*

MIN JIANG
Goodwood Park Hotel
Tel: 1800-737-5337
Try the camphor-and-tea-smoked duck, and the Szechuan pancake for dessert. *Expensive*

Teochew

PEACH BLOSSOMS
Marina Mandarin Hotel
Tel: 338-3388
Rich decor and beautifully-presented dishes. The restaurant also serves Cantonese dishes. *Expensive*

BAN SENG
The Riverwalk
20 Upper Circular
Tel: 533-1471, 534-3637
Changed little since the old days. For dessert, try *oh nee*, a sweet yam paste with nuts. *Moderate*

Hokkien

BENG HIANG
112 Amoy Street
Tel: 221-6684, 221-6695
One of the best. Not very atmospheric but the fish maw soup and roast suckling piglet are especially good. *Moderate*

BENG THIN HOON KEE
#05-02 OCBC Centre
Chulia Street
Tel: 533-7708
The Hokkien fried mee and oyster omelette are recommended highly. *Moderate*

Hunan

CHARMING GARDEN
Novotel Orchid Inn
Tel: 251-8149
Overlooks a pool and garden. Try the steamed red tilapia, a delicate fish with crispy soya bean crumb topping. *Expensive*

Chinese herbal tea 'cools' the system

Hakka

MOI KONG
22 Murray Street
Tel: 221-7758, 224-9923
Sample the Hakka speciality, *yong tau foo*. *Inexpensive*

Hainanese

MOOI CHIN
#01-05 Funan Centre
Tel: 339-7766, 339-3611
Feast on Hainanese pork chops, mutton soup and pomfret *sambal* in this charming restaurant. *Inexpensive*

Chinese Vegetarian

MIAO YI VEGETARIAN RESTAURANT
#03-01/02 Coronation
Shopping Plaza
Tel: 467-1331
For the vegetarian who loves local flavours. *Inexpensive*

North Indian

DELHI RESTAURANT
60 Race Course Road
Tel: 296-4585
A cosy restaurant serving tasty North Indian cuisine at reasonable prices. Reservations are advisable. *Moderate*

MOGHUL MAHAL
#01-11 Colombo Court
Tel: 338-7794, 338-6907
The one that Northern Indians go to. *Expensive*

MOTI MAHAL
18 Murray Street
Tel: 221-4338
Considered by many to be the best in Southeast Asia. *Moderate*

South Indian

ANNALAKSHMI
#02-10 Excelsior Hotel
Tel: 339-9993, 339-3007
Exquisite setting to match the fine vegetarian fare. Try the lunch and dinner buffets. *Moderate*

KOMALA VILAS
76 Serangoon Road
Tel: 293-6980
In Little India, simple but good vegetarian fare. *Inexpensive*

BANANA LEAF APOLO
54 Race Course Road
Tel: 293-8682
Spicy fare served on banana leaves. Use of fingers is *de rigeur*. *Inexpensive*

Malay/Indonesian

DESA KARTIKA
#05-32 Ngee Ann City
Tel: 732-7372
Plush Indonesian restaurant with a warm and cosy ambience. The good service and atmosphere almost makes up for avarege fare. *Expensive*

RENDEZVOUS
Hotel Rendezvous
Tel: 339-7508
A firm favourite with the city's lunch-time crowds. Recently moved to its original 1970s premises – now a modern hotel. *Moderate*

THE RICE TABLE
#02-09 International Building
360 Orchard Road
Tel: 835-3783
Convenient location on Orchard Road, offering great value lunch and dinner buffets. *Moderate*

RIVERSIDE INDONESIAN RESTAURANT
#01-04 Riverside Point
30 Riverside Road
Tel: 535-0383
Riverside location opposite Clarke Quay adds flavour to the restaurant's ambience. Known for its grilled dishes. *Moderate*

SANUR
#04-17/18 Centrepoint
Tel: 734-2192
Very popular and invariably crowded. The *gado gado* salad, beef *rendang* and *tahu telur* are highly recommended. *Moderate*

TAMBUAH MAS
#05-14 Shaw Centre
1 Scott Road
Tel: 733-3333
A favourite with locals. Try *tahu telur*, crispy fried *gurami* fish and barbecued squid. *Moderate*

Nonya

BLUE GINGER
97 Tanjong Pagar Road
Tel: 222-3928
Upscale shophouse restaurant with excellent service. The food is almost as good as the gorgeous setting. *Expensive*

NONYA AND BABA RESTAURANT
262/264 River Valley Road
Tel: 734-1382/6
Traditional setting is ideal for authentic Peranakan dishes. *Moderate*

Seafood

LONG BEACH SEAFOOD RESTAURANT
Car Park A, Planet Marina
Marina South
Tel: 445-8833
Evenings only, for some of the best chilli crabs in town. *Moderate*

SEAFOOD INTERNATIONAL MARKET & RESTAURANT
Big Splash
902 East Coast Parkway
Tel: 345-1211/2/3
The supermarket-style seafood display will have your mouth watering. Choose what you want and have it cooked in one of 30 different ways. *Moderate*

Japanese

KEYAKI
Pan Pacific Hotel
Tel: 336-8111
A lovely water garden leads to the restaurant where excellent *teppanyaki* and other Japanese fare is served. *Expensive*

NANBENTEI
#05-132 Far East Plaza
Tel: 733-5666
Charming restaurant with good food at reasonable prices. Excellent *miso* dressing for salads. *Moderate*

Thai

LEMON GRASS
#05-02A The Heeren
260 Orchard Road
Tel: 736-1998
An above average restaurant with reasonably-priced dishes. *Moderate*

THANG YING RESTAURANT
Amara Hotel
165 Tanjong Pagar Road
Tel: 222-4688
The resident chef worked previously for the Thai royal family, so expect to pay for it. *Expensive*

East-West Fusion

COMPASS ROSE RESTAURANT
70th Floor
Westin Stamford Hotel
Tel: 338-8585
Spectacular vistas with cuisine blending Asian and Western flavours. *Expensive.*

THE MEZZA 9
Grand Hyatt Hotel
Tel: 738-1234
A new-concept huge restaurant serving Chinese, Japanese and Western food. Attracts a trendy crowd. *Expensive*

TRADER VIC'S
5th Floor, Hotel New Otani
Tel: 433-8890
Funky Polynesian atmosphere and tropical tipples. The exotic food is just as good. *Expensive*

Continental

LATOUR
Shangri-La Hotel
Tel: 737-3644
The affordable lunchtime semi-*a la carte* buffet is one of the best in town. Reservations recommended. *Expensive*

MORTON'S OF CHICAGO
Oriental Hotel
Tel: 339-3740
Probably the most expensive western restaurant in Singapore but also very good. Recommended are its Porterhouse steak, broiled salmon and shrimp Alexander. *Expensive*

THE RAFFLES GRILL
Raffles Hotel
Tel: 337-1886
Sophisticated ambience and cuisine make for a special evening. But stop at the Long Bar first for a pre-dinner Singapore Sling. *Expensive*

Dig into Indian dhosai

MARCHE
#01-03 The Heeren
Tel: 737-6996
From the Movenpick chain, a very European food-court type of restaurant. *Moderate*

French

LA BRASSERIE
Marco Polo Hotel
Tel: 474-7141
Everyone's favourite. For dessert, try the white truffle chocolate cake. *Expensive*

SALUT
27 Tanjong Pagar Road
Tel: 225-7555
Intimate ambience and excellent food combining the best of France and Italy. *Expensive*

VIS-À-VIS
12 Chun Tin Road
Tel: 468-7433
A delightful little restaurant in the suburbs. *Moderate*

English

THE GORDON GRILL
Goodwood Park Hotel
Tel: 235-8637
Innovative British cuisine like smoked duck breast with hazelnut dressing. *Expensive*

FOSTERS OLDE
Palais Renaissance
390 Orchard Road
Tel: 737-8939
Traditional British fare. Try the cream tea from 3–6pm. *Moderate*

American

DAN RYAN'S CHICAGO GRILL
#B1-01 Tanglin Mall
Tel: 738-2800
American-sized portions served by a friendly crew. *Moderate*

HARD ROCK CAFE
50 Cuscaden Road
Tel: 235-5232
Quick, delightful service as you freak out to the great sounds. *Moderate*

PLANET HOLLYWOOD
#02-02 Liat Towers
541 Orchard Road
Ho-hum food but fun atmosphere. The kids will love this place. *Moderate*

Italian

RISTORANTE BOLOGNA
Marina Mandarin Hotel
Tel: 338-3388
A trio will serenade you as you tuck into its excellent Italian specialities. Do not miss the *zabaglione al marsala*, prepared to the beat of music at your table. *Expensive*

PREGO
Level 1, The Westin Plaza
Tel: 338-8585
This bright, cheery restaurant serves above average Italian fare. *Expensive*

DA PAOLO
80 Club Street
Tel: 224-7081
Exquisite pastas served in the very *chi chi* atmosphere of a restored shophouse. There is a second outlet at Tanjong Pagar Road with a very different atmosphere. *Expensive*

Shopping

From shiny new shopping centres to the musty shophouses of Chinatown, there is a selection of merchandise possibly unrivalled in the world. Goods imported from all over the globe vie with locally-made bargains. Shops are generally open seven days a week from 10am to at least 9pm. The main problems are where to start, and when to stop.

Bargain only in the smaller shops and let the salesperson know if you intend to pay by credit card, as he or she will have to factor the surcharge into the price. Remember, if you have bargained at length and agreed on the price, you are under a moral obligation to buy!

There is a 3 percent Goods and Services Tax (GST) on all your purchases in Singapore, but visitors who spend S$300 or more in the same shop or shops belonging to the same retail chain displaying the 'Tax Free Shopping' sticker can apply for a GST refund (see *Practical Information* for details).

The Singapore Tourism Board has authorised certain shops to display its Gold Circle's Promise of Excellence sticker as a symbol of its recommendation. However, if you do have any complaints, the

Antique hunting

Consumer Association of Singapore (CASE, tel: 270-5433) is there to help. Alternatively, you can turn to the Small Claims Tribunals (tel: 435-5937) which have a fast track procedure for visitors. A S$10 fee is charged and where possible cases are heard within a day.

What to Buy

Cameras and Audio Equipment

Prices are attractive, particularly for photographic equipment and the latest walkman or portable CD player. CDs and tapes are often cheaper here than elsewhere too. It's a good idea to get an international guarantee, but if you want to take a risk on directly imported goods intended only for the local market, you can save on the price. If you don't see what you want in the shop, ask, because it can be fetched for you in no time.

Computer Equipment

Everything for the computer buff, local and imported, from the latest laptop to a wide selection of software. Don't forget to check the voltage.

Watches and Jewellery

Watches are sold tax-free, and the choice is never-ending, from a lifetime's investment in a Rolex to a cheap plastic fun Swatch.

Singapore glitters, and it is likely to be with gold, probably the very pure 22K and 24K yellow gold that the locals tend to favour. Indian jewellers in Serangoon Road sell intricate pieces in bright gold. Live orchid blooms – sold under the Risis brand – coated with pure 22K gold to preserve their beauty can be worn as rings, earrings, pendants or bracelets.

The selection of jewellery here is mind-boggling. The Chinese love jade, and from the paler nephrite to the bright green jadite, all kinds of pretty pendants, rings and earrings are made. Lovely statues are sculptured in jade, often of Chinese deities. These are also carved in ivory or whalebone. Ivory trade is now banned worldwide so be careful in case you cannot bring these into your country.

Mikimoto pearls from Japan are laid out in rows, and freshwater pearls of all colours are cheap enough to buy several strands to twist into a choker. You can even choose a gemstone and make up your own design, or rely on the expertise of the great jewellery designers in the world, such as Cartier and Bvlgari.

Fashion

Designer shops are everywhere for the fashion conscious, but you can always have that special dress copied, or a suit made-to-measure by one of the many tailors.

There is lovely *batik* from Malaysia and Indonesia as well as locally printed *batik* with orchid motifs. You can find silks from China, Thailand, India and Malaysia.

For the fashion conscious

There's a whole range of shoes, from Bally to attractive locally made footwear which look great, even though they may not be as durable as imports. You'll find handbags and belts of all shapes, sizes and prices too. Goods made from alligator, crocodile and snake skins are good buys, but again check with your embassy in case there is an import ban in your country.

Antiques and Asian Exotica

As Singapore is a trading port in the heart of Asia, the selection of artefacts from Bangkok to Borneo and beyond is quite extraordinary. You can find baskets and lovely shell dishes and lamps from the Philippines. From Japan come miniature masterpieces of design; tiny sewing or writing compacts the size of a credit card, as well as lacquerware and delicate porcelain. What about silk photoframes, ties and jackets from Thailand, Indian *papier mâché* and brassware, and sandlewood carvings and gems from Sri Lanka? Then there's a whole range of items by Selangor Pewter from Malaysia, and Buddha figurines from Burma and Thailand. If you can't carry it all, then ship it back home in a Korean camphorwood chest.

For the connoisseur, prints and maps as well as old editions of books on the region can be found, and also old porcelain, figurines and coins. A certificate of antiquity will be given with a genuine antique purchase.

Oriental Carpets

You will find an enormous selection of beautiful Oriental carpets, from tribal rugs to exquisite silk carpets in glorious colours and intricate designs. When buying, look at the workmanship: the dying, knotting and clipping in the finished carpet are important criteria. The more knots per square centimetre, the finer (and more expensive) the carpet, so turn it over and have a look at the back.

Buy what you will be happy with, but beware of being charged for an antique piece unless that is what you really want. Take the carpet into daylight to see the colours, and take your time to choose.

Things Chinese

Colourful cloisonnéware from China is made into everything from pens and earrings to lampstands. Exquisite lace table linen whether as cloths or mats look elegant for dinner parties. Embroidered Mandarin sleeves, old and new, look wonderful framed, or set under the glass of a coffee table. China produces china too – ceramics, old, new and reproductions, for display or daily use, can be found. Paper lamps, fans, carvings and silk paintings are pretty and easy to transport home.

Where to Buy

If it's shopping in Singapore, it has to be Orchard Road. Right at the top end, just before Orchard Road proper, is my favourite haunt, the **Tanglin Shopping Centre** which has become something of an antique, carpets and fine arts centre. On the first floor is **CT Hoo**, which has the widest selection of pearls in Singapore. Don't miss the sumptuous carpets at **Caravan International, Mohammed Akhtar** and **Hassan's Carpets**. The last two are still run by the families who founded them. For instance, Mohammed Akhtar has been in the business since 1905 and both companies are run by second- and third-generation family members. Just along the corridor is **Renee Hoy Galleries**, where you'll find exquisite Asian treasures, and any questions you ask will be patiently answered. There are antique and fine art shops on all three shopping levels. Of special note is the remarkable range of antique prints, old maps and rare books that can be found in **Antiques of the Orient** on level 2, and there is an excellent choice of modern books on the region in **Select Books** on

Carpets for sale

level 3. Browse around and you'll find fascinating artefacts from all over Asia, jewellery and garment shops.

Then go straight on to Bangkok's famous **Jim Thompson's** at the Orchard Parade hotel from where you can cross over to the **Delfi Orchard** building for Royal Selangor pewterware, Waterford crystals and Wedgwood porcelain.

Orchard Towers beckons with jewellery and silk, antiques and shoes, and some of the cheapest and widest range of electronic equipment, cameras, watches and binoculars. Next door, **Palais Renaissance** houses exquisite boutiques like DKNY, Gianni Versace and Prada.

If you need to appease your tykes in tow, cross over to Toys R' Us, the world's largest toy store chain in **Forum The Shopping Mall**. You'll also find boutiques specialising in children's clothes here. Then browse through the **Hilton Shopping Gallery**, next down the road, where Cartier and other top names may tempt you.

At the traffic lights, cross over to the **Isetan Scotts**. Apart from affordable clothes, cosmetics, shoes and bags, women shoppers with children will find the children's department, complete with nursery and play area, a real boon. Opposite Isetan Scotts on Orchard Road is **Wheelock Place** with the Borders bookshop as anchor tenant and a Marks and Spencer branch at the basement level.

An underpass leads to **Tangs**, full of Asian temptations ranging from snack foods (in the basement) to an excellent selection of local and foreign ready-to-wear labels. **Lucky Plaza** next door is for the camera and watch enthusiast.

Return to the underpass and cross over to **Wisma Atria**, an airy complex with all manner of shops and boutiques, including another **Isetan**. The huge complex next door is **Ngee Ann City**, Southeast Asia's largest shopping mall, with **Takashimaya** department store as

In the heart of Orchard Road – Centrepoint

its main tenant and numerous shops selling designer labels as well as **Harrods** from London.

On the other side of the road, you may browse through **Promenade**, the **Paragon** and the **Esprit** store. Further down is **The Heeren** with a huge HMV store, followed by smaller malls like **Orchard Emerald** and on to **Centrepoint**. This is home to Britain's Marks and Spencer, called **St Michael's** here, as well as Singapore's original department store **Robinson's** and a host of other shops, including The Body Shop, Mondi, Mothercare and Bruno Magli. Next to Centrepoint, explore **Orchard Point** where you can find clothes for the office as well as for the weekend.

Outside the Orchard Road area, **People's Park Complex** in Chinatown offers bales of all kinds of fabric. **Pidemco Centre**, not far away, is the place for local gold and jewellery.

The **Funan Centre** in Hill Street and **Sim Lim Square** in Rochor Road are full of electronic appliances, and computers software and hardware.

Holland Shopping Centre in **Holland Village**, a little further out of town, is the expat ladies' haunt, and you'll find a wide range of bags, shoes, jewellery and clothes from batik to comfortable casuals. Solve all your gift and souvenir problems in **Lim's Arts and Crafts**, a real treasure trove.

Go down Lorong Liput and explore **Lorong Mambong** behind the shopping centre, a lively little street with a traditional wet market on one side, and baskets spilling out of shops on the other. Rummage there to find hand-woven baskets and porcelain ware; superb carpets at **Hedger's** and clothes at bargain prices at the **Factory Outlet**.

Just along Holland Road at Jalan Jelita is **Jelita Cold Storage**. Go upstairs and find yourself in India, amid pre- and post-colonial furniture and fascinating artefacts in **Ji-Reen Home Boutique**. **Jessica Art N' Craft** is nearby, a lovely Oriental boutique to explore. For furniture, antiques and cane, the shops in **Watten Estate** along Bukit Timah are a must.

Arab Street, off Beach Road, is another great place for hand-woven baskets, *batik* and all things Islamic, **Serangoon Road** for goods from India, and of course **Chinatown** for Chinese souvenirs of every kind from paper umbrellas to ginseng. If you have a penchant for Ming Dynasty replicas, head for **Ming Village** at 32 Pandan Road in the west of the island. This is the largest remaining pottery centre and still makes replicas of museum masterpieces using traditional methods, all entirely by hand. On the same grounds is the **Pewter Museum** which has over 1,000 beautifully crafted pieces on display. Both are open daily 9am to 5.30pm (tel: 265-7711) with regular demonstrations by the artists.

Calendar of Special Events

Given the mix of races and religions, it's not surprising that Singapore's annual calendar is jam-packed with festivals throughout the year. Although the precise dates of ethnic festivals vary because they are based on the lunar calendar, most can be confined to one or two specific months.

The only exception is the Muslim festival of **Hari Raya Puasa** which is advanced by a month or so each year. The festival celebrates the end of *Ramadan* where no food or drink is consumed from dawn to dusk. During this month, visit Busorrah Street where food stalls are set up each evening for Muslims to break their fast. Over at Geylang, in the eastern part of Singapore, a festive market-like atmosphere pervades in the evenings when the coloured lights are switched on and vendors in makeshift stalls compete for customers with their food and wares. The other Muslim festival celebrated with a public holiday here is **Hari Raya Haji**. This is a more solemn occasion which marks the sacrifices made by Muslims who undertake the pilgrimage to Mecca and the mandatory giving of alms to the needy.

If you plan to have your trip coincide with a major festival, it's best

A devotee at Thaipusam

to check with a Singapore embassy or consulate in your country. When in Singapore, check with the Singapore Tourism Board (tel: 1800-334-1334/6 or 1800-738-3778/9), or simply check a local calendar.

JANUARY/FEBRUARY

Weeks before **Chinese Lunar New Year**, Chinatown is decked out in coloured lights, and red and gold decorations. Pussy willow and *kumquat* trees are sold, and gifts of oranges and money in special *hong bao* envelopes are given, all accompanied by the drumming and prancing of lion dancers. A colourful parade with dances and floats called Chingay is held about this time.

Also during this period is the Indian harvest festival of **Ponggal.**

104

In Indian homes, a pot of rice is allowed to boil over to symbolise prosperity, and food is offered to the gods in the Sri Perumal Temple in Serangoon Road.

Then comes the startling Indian festival of **Thaipusam**. Devotees carry enormous arched structures called *kavadis* along a 3-km (2-mile) route from the Sri Perumal Temple in Serangoon Road to the Chettiar Temple in Tank Road. The *kavadis* are decorated with peacock feathers and are held in place by hooks and skewers which pierce the body. No blood is drawn though as the faithful have prepared themselves for the ordeal with weeks of prayer and fasting.

Twice a year, in February and September, Chinese mediums in a trance announce the **Birthday of the Monkey God**, celebrated at the Monkey God Temple in Seng Poh Road.

MARCH/APRIL

Good Friday, which precedes Easter, is observed at many churches in Singapore. In Catholic churches, the crucifixion of Jesus Christ is enacted, and candle-lit processions are held at the St Joseph's Church (Portuguese Mission) in Victoria Street and the Novena Church in Thomson Road. Expect crowds and dripping candle wax on your clothes.

Also around this time is **Qing Ming**. Ancestral graves are tidied for the occasion and incense papers, hell-money and paper gifts are burnt.

MAY/JUNE

Vesak Day commemorates Buddha's birth, enlightenment and death. Prayer and meditation takes place at the temples, followed by the release of caged birds.

Ritual celebrations for the **Birthday of the Third Prince**, a child god, are held in Chinese temples in May, with mediums in trance cutting themselves with swords and smearing the blood onto paper for devotees.

The **Dragon Boat Festival** in June sees exciting races between teams from all over the world paddling across Marina Bay. It is held in remembrance of the poet Qu Yuan who drowned himself in protest against political corruption in China.

AUGUST/SEPTEMBER

August is an important month. To celebrate **National Day** on 9 August, a parade is held either at the Padang or National Stadium; the evening ending with fireworks.

Then it's the start of the Chinese **Hungry Ghosts** month. The Chinese believe that the gates of hell open during this month and the ghosts

Chettiar Temple

visit our world. Incense sticks and hell-money are burned and food is offered to placate the ghosts.

The **Mooncake Festival** which takes place soon after the Hungry Ghosts month brings delicious moon-shaped pastries with fillings of lotus paste, red bean paste, nuts or preserved duck eggs. A lantern display lights up the Chinese Garden.

OCTOBER

In October, Little India and Indian homes glow with lighted oil lamps and garlands in celebration of **Deepavali**, when the powers of light triumph over darkness. This is also the most important Hindu festival for the local Indian community. Prayers are recited in temples and statues of deities are carried round the grounds.

During this month, Indian temples are also the venue for classical dance and musical performances in honour of Dhurga, Lakshmi and Saraswathi, the consorts of the Hindu Trinity for the **Festival of Navarathiri**.

The **Thimithi** festival, also in October, is something to watch out for. Fire-walking in honour of the goddess Draupadi, heroine of the *Mahabharata* epic, who walked on fire to prove her chastity, takes place in the Sri Mariamman Temple in South Bridge Road.

Kusu Island is the destination for Chinese and Muslim pilgrims from mid-October to mid-November. According to legend, two fishermen were carried to safety on the island on the back of a giant turtle which rescued them after their boat sank. Of different faiths, one built the Tua Pek Kong Taoist Temple, the other the Muslim Keramat hilltop shrine.

The **Festival of the Nine Emperor Gods**, during which the divine powers are said to cure all ills and bestow good fortune on their nine-day visit to earth, is celebrated with *wayangs* (Chinese operas) and a great procession with the effigies of the gods borne aloft in sedan chairs.

NOVEMBER/DECEMBER

Orchard Road lights up for **Christmas** on 25 December, and the year winds up with carol-singing in the streets and parties everywhere.

Heralding the advent of Christmas

PRACTICAL information

Orchids: Singapore's pride

GETTING THERE

By Air

Landing in Singapore's **Changi Airport** is a luxurious experience. Constantly polled the world's best airport in various readership surveys, Terminal 1 and Terminal 2 – which are linked by the Sky Train – share an ever-increasing load of passenger and air traffic. All major airlines land here, baggage handling is quick and there are always taxis waiting to whisk arriving passengers to their hotels.

By Sea

More and more cruise liners are stopping off at Singapore, sailing in from Europe, Hong Kong, America and India to what is now the busiest port in the world. Most visitors arrive at one of three terminals of the Singapore Cruise Centre in World Trade Centre.

By Road

There are good roads into Singapore through Malaysia, from Ipoh and Kuala Lumpur on the west coast, and Kota Bahru on the east. The fastest route from Malaysia is via the North-South Highway which takes about four hours to drive from Kuala Lumpur (KL) to Singapore. Depending on which route you take, entry into Singapore is either through the Woodlands Causeway in the north of Singapore or the new Tuas Second Link Causeway in the west of the island. Note that the latter is less prone to traffic jams.

By Rail

A railway line links Singapore to Kuala Lumpur (KL) and Bangkok, with daily trains leaving Bangkok at 3.15pm and arriving in KL at 8pm the following night. From KL, departures at 7.45am, 2.30pm and 10.30pm arrive in Singapore at 2pm, 9pm and 7am the following day respectively. To check schedules, routes, fares, including rail connections from Singapore, contact the Railway Station at Keppel Road, tel: 222-5165.

The other (and much more expensive) way of arriving by rail is to book a seat on the Eastern & Orient Express which plies between Bangkok, KL and Singapore. The 1,943-km (1,205-mile) route from Bangkok via KL and on to

Finger Pier Container Port

Singapore and vice versa takes three days and two nights. Fares start at US$1,300 per person, while the 8-hour route from KL to Singapore starts from US$550 per person, with all meals included in the fare. For reservations call tel: 392-3500 in Singapore; tel: (171) 805-5100 in UK; tel: (800) 524-2420 in USA; and tel: 1-800-331-429 toll free in Australia.

TRAVEL ESSENTIALS

Climate & When to Visit

The average daily temperature is 26.7°C (80°F), often rising to around 30°C (87°F) during the day, and cooling only to around 23°C (75°F) at night. Humidity varies between 64 and 96 percent.

The Northeast monsoon blows from December to March, and the Southwest from June to September, making it breezier during these months. Spectacular thunderstorms occur frequently between the monsoons, in April and May, and October and November. The average rainfall is 237cm (93in).

The slightly cooler rainy season lasts roughly from November to January – winter time in Europe, North America and Japan – when the long tropical days here are especially welcome to travellers from these countries. Frequently, the skies open suddenly on everything and everyone, often causing traffic jams and making it harder to hail a taxi. But it's usually all over quickly, leaving everything sparkling in the sunlight.

June and July are warmer months, more conducive to lying at the poolside or browsing in the air-conditioned shopping centres than to sightseeing.

Visas

As long as you have a valid passport, onward travel reservations and adequate finance, you do not need a visa to enter Singapore. However, citizens of China, India and Vietnam, among others, require a visa. You will normally be given a one-month visa if arriving by air, or a two-week visa if coming overland from Malaysia, so remember to check the date and renew if necessary at the Immigration Office, 10 Kallang Road. For details, call tel: 391-6100 or the toll-free line at 1800-391-6400.

Vaccination

A Yellow Fever vaccination is necessary if arriving from an infected country.

Money Matters

The local currency consists of notes in $2, $5, $10, $20, $50, $100, $500, $1,000 and $10,000 denominations. Coins are in denomination of 1, 5, 10, 20, 50 cents and $1.

There are no restrictions on the amount of currency you can bring into the country. Generally, banks and licensed money changers offer better rates than hotels.

International charge and credit cards are widely accepted in Singapore. For travellers' cheques and foreign currency transactions, it is advisable to deal with the banks on weekdays. Some banks do not handle such transactions on Saturdays.

Dress for the tropics

What to Wear

Loose, casual clothes, preferably made of cotton and other natural fabrics, are more comfortable in the heat. Shorts and tees are quite acceptable in many places. Ties are only worn for formal occasions, and jackets almost never, although some clubs and discos do have a strict dress code.

Electricity

Electrical supply is on a 220–240 volt, 50 Hz system. Most hotels have transformers for 110–120 volt, 60 Hz appliances.

Airport Tax

A charge of S$15 for passengers departing on international flights is levied at the airport. It is possible to buy these coupons at most hotels, travel agents and airline offices.

GETTING ACQUAINTED

Geography

The Republic of Singapore consists of the main island, about 616sq km (238sq miles) in area, and 58 other islets. Located at the southern tip of Peninsular Malaysia, it is joined to the latter by the Johor–Singapore Causeway (or Woodlands Causeway) and the new Tuas Second Link Causeway which opened in 1998. Land is scarce, and the shape of the island has changed over the years through land reclamation. The highest point is Bukit Timah Hill at 162½m (580ft) with most of the main island less than 15m (50ft) above sea level.

Time

Singapore is eight hours ahead of Greenwich Mean Time.

Tipping

You don't have to tip for good service in Singapore, and in general this holds good as most hotel and restaurant bills come with a 10 percent service charge and a 4 percent government tax. But if these are absent, tips are appreciated.

Tourist Information

There's a wealth of free literature at the airport, hotels, shopping centres and tourist attractions, all making life easy for the visitor.

The Singapore Tourism Board has two information counters if you require help or information:
Ground floor, Tourism Court, 1 Orchard Spring Lane, tel: 1800-738-3778/9. Open Monday–Saturday, 8.30am–6pm.

#02-34 Raffles Hotel Arcade, 328 North Bridge Road, tel: 1800-334-1334/69. Open daily 9.30am–9.30pm.

Alternatively, check out the STB website at www.newasia.singapore.com

Bus Tours

If you prefer not to track down Singapore's attractions on your own, book yourself on a bus tour. Several reliable companies operate interesting half- and full-day visits of the various sights with guides to provide the commentary: Gray Line Tours (tel: 331-8244); RMG Tours (tel: 220-1661); Singapore Sightseeing Tour East (tel: 332-3755). If you prefer a personal guide who can tailor-make tours to wherever you please, on foot, by taxi or limousine or in a bus, contact Geraldine Lowe-Ismail (tel: 737-5250). She charges S$60 for an hour of her time, but if you join a tour she has already organised, it will cost S$35 for half a day. Another reliable contact is Felicia Teo (tel: 266-5260).

Goods and Services Tax

A GST of 3 percent is charged on most goods and services purchased in Singapore. The good news for visitors is that you may apply for a tax refund if you've purchased goods worth S$300 and more in a shop or department store that participates in the GST Tourist Refund Scheme. In order to qualify for the refund, make sure that you've purchased the items in the same shop or shops belonging to the same retail chain. All participating shops will have a clearly displayed TAX REFUND sticker. Fill out a Claims form available at the shop where you purchased your goods and present it, together with your purchased items, to the customs officers at the airport on departure. Return the customs-stamped forms to the shop where you purchased your goods and the refund will be mailed to you either by cheque in Singapore dollars or credited into your credit card account.

How Not to Offend

Good behaviour in Singapore is law-enforced; clear signs explain what to do and what not to do. Littering could cost you up to S$1,000; smoking in government offices, air-conditioned restaurants, cinemas, supermarkets etc, S$500; and if you're caught without a seat belt, it means forking out extra money. There is a huge misconception that you will be fined for chewing gum in Singapore. This is not true. The fine is enforced only for the import and sale of chewing gum. If you bring a couple of sticks into the country for personal consumption, rest assured you will not get into trouble with the authorities.

You won't be fined, but remember to take off your shoes when you enter a mosque or Indian temple or an Asian's house. When with Muslims, neither eat nor offer anything with your left hand.

In general, Singapore is cosmopolitan, and courteous behaviour will make sure you don't offend, even if you are unfamiliar with the finer points of Asian etiquette. To learn more, look out for a fascinating book by JoAnn Meriwether Craig called *Culture Shock in Singapore* which explains the mores of this city.

GETTING AROUND

Electronic Road Pricing

To reduce traffic flow in the city, all vehicles entering the Central Business District (CBD) between 7.30am and 7pm and on the expressways during the morning peak hours between 7.30am and 9.30am, are required to pay a toll. Called Electronic Road Pricing (ERP), the fee is automatically deducted from a cash card slotted into the In-Vehicle Unit (IU) that all vehicles (including rental cars and taxis) in Singapore are outfitted with. Stored-value cash cards can be purchased from any post office or petrol station in Singapore and their value can be topped up once the reserve amount is depleted. Most car rental companies will also sell you cash cards if you rent a car from them. This being Singapore, there is a fine of S$30 each time you pass through a gantry point without a cash card in your IU. You have been warned!

From the airport

If you've arrived at the airport without arranging to have a hotel pick you up, don't despair. There are four types of transport from the airport: private car, taxi, Maxicab, and public bus. The last is no good if you have heavy luggage with you. The taxi stand for both Terminal 1 and 2 is situated on the same level as the Arrival Hall. The 20-minute trip (barring peak hour traffic jams) to the city on the East Coast Parkway (ECP) should cost about S$15–18 plus a S$3 surcharge. In addition, during operating hours, ERP charges kick in when the taxi passes gantry points in the ECP and the CBD.

Alternatively, take one of the Airport Shuttle Service's Maxicabs which carry a maximum of six passengers at a time. These pick up pasengers just outside the Arrival Halls of Terminals 1 and 2 and operate between 9am and 11pm (half hourly 9am–6pm and every 15 minutes 6–11pm). Fares are $7 (adult) and $5 (child) and you can ask to be dropped off anywhere in the city, including MRT stations.

Taxis

By far the easiest way to see Singapore is to take one of the more than 15,000 taxis – either Comfort, CityCab or TIBS – which provide excellent service. Most drivers speak or understand English. Still, make sure the driver knows where you want to go first before starting off. Generally, taxis can be hailed off the streets or at taxi stands in the city. However, during peak hours and when in rains, empty taxis are a rare sight. So it is better to call ahead and book one.

All taxis seat four passengers and are metered with fares beginning at S$2.40 for the first 1km or less, plus

PLEASE DO NOT LITTER

LITTERING CARRIES A MAXIMUM FINE OF $1000

Trishaws are a cool way to travel

10 cents for every 240m travelled. There's a 50 percent surcharge between midnight and 6am. If the taxi enters the CBD between 7.30am and 7pm Monday to Friday and 8.30am–1pm Saturday, and the expressways between 7.30am and 9.30am Monday to Friday, there are ERP surcharges of between 35 cents and S$1. In the CBD area, there is a surcharge of S$1.50 if you ride a taxi from 4.30pm to 7pm Monday to Friday and 11.30am to 2pm on Saturday. To make matters confusing, if you hire a taxi during peak hours outside of the CBD area, ie between 7.30am and 9.30am Monday to Saturday, 4.30pm and 7pm Monday to Friday and between 11.30am and 2pm Saturday, a surcharge of S$1 applies. Be prepared to fork out another 10 percent on top of the fare if you pay by credit card. Booking a taxi by phone for immediate use will cost you S$3.20, or $5.20 if you book one at least 30 minutes in advance.

If you're sufficiently confused by now, do what most Singaporeans do: just pay what the taxi driver tells you to! Most taxi drivers are honest chaps but if you feel you've been ripped off, call the following numbers to complain; Comfort: tel: 458-2555; CityCab: tel: 553-3877; and TIBS: tel: 483-3225.

Car Hire

Avis (tel: 737-1668) and Budget (tel: 532-4442) offer both self-drive and chauffeur-driven cars. You will need a valid driving licence. Make sure that the car has an IU and that the cash card

MRT – fast, modern and efficient

inserted before you drive off. Driving is on the left and seat belts are compulsory.

Trishaws

Although mainly used by tourist groups, you can hire a trishaw on your own, but make sure you agree on the destination and fare first. A tour of the city, lasting 20–30 minutes will cost about S$25–30. Find them at Bras Basah Road in front of the Singapore Art Museum or else enquire at your hotel reception desk.

Buses

You can get about just everywhere on the bus in Singapore. Timetables sold in bookshops and bus terminals indicate the buses to and from the main attractions. Buses (SBS and TIBS) operate from 6am to 11.45pm and fares start from 60 cents. There are no conductors on board so make sure you have the exact fare. For easy travelling, buy a **Singapore Explorer** ticket from selected TransitLink offices in the MRT stations and hotels. It costs S$5 for a one-day ticket or S$12 for a three-day ticket. A tourist map comes with the ticket. For more info, call the SBS customer hotline at 1800-287-2727.

MRT

Singapore's **Mass Rapid Transit** (MRT) is the envy of commuters everywhere. Strict laws and fines prohibiting eating and littering ensure spotless stations and carriages. A third of the system runs underground, enabling some of the stations to serve as emergency bunkers if ever there is a need for them.

The system is simple and easy to use; just remember that you need your ticket to leave the station at your destination. Trains run every 3–8 minutes and operate from 6am to midnight.

Visitors may find it useful to buy a stored-value card, which for a minimum of S$12 (including a S$2 deposit) gives you access to all MRT trains and buses (just remember to slot the card face down for bus rides) for up to the value of S$10. Any unused fare and deposit can be refunded at TransitLink offices in the MRT stations. There is also a S$7 tourist card which doubles as an attractive souvenir. It is valid for 120 days and allows usage up to a value of S$6. No refund is given on the remaining value of the ticket. Should your last trip exceed the remaining value, you will have to pay the difference. Inquire at MRT information counters.

Singapore Trolley

These brown and marron trams ply between the main hotels and tourist attractions from the Botanic Gardens to Tanjong Pagar and even to World Trade Centre, the jump-off point for Sentosa. Unlimited travel all day costs S$9 (adult), S$7 (child). A point-to-point S$3 fare is also available. Buy your ticket from your hotel concierge or direct from the driver. Brochures are available in most hotels and tourist destinations, or call 227-8218 for more information.

Maps

There are several excellent free maps which have detailed sections of specific parts of the city, like Chinatown for instance. These can be picked up at Changi Airport and major hotels. Most bookshops stock larger maps of Singapore and Malaysia. Then there's the *Secret Map of Singapore* (available in bookshops) which gives colourful and graphical summaries of the major places of interest in Singapore.

ACCOMMODATION

Hotels in Singapore rate among the best in the world in terms of service, comfort and amenities. The Shangri-La for instance has been rated very highly by international business executives for the past decade. The hotels here are listed in alphabetical order. Do check with the respective reservations desk for special promotion rates and especially during the low season. Note that prices are subject to 10 percent service charge, 3 percent GST and 1 percent cess.

If you arrive at Changi airport without booking a room, head for the Singapore Hotel Association counters (open daily 7.30am–11.30pm) at Terminal 1 and 2 and the staff will help you with hotel reservations. Rack rates for standard double rooms are as follows:

$$$ = $300 and above
$$ = $199–$200
$ = $100 and below

AMARA
165 Tanjong Pagar Road
Tel: 224-4488
Business hotel close to the heart of Singapore's financial district. Little to recommend it except that its Thanying restaurant serves excellent Thai food. *$$*

ANA
16 Nassim Hill
Tel: 732-1222
The hospitality arm of All Nippon Airways, a quality business-class hotel (456 rooms) situated atop a ridge, close to Singapore's embassy row. *$$*

CONCORDE
317 Outram Road
Tel: 733-0188
Good value for money and close to Chinatown and riverside areas. *$$*

CROWN PRINCE
270 Orchard Road
Tel: 732-1111
Excellent for shopping as it's located in the heart of Orchard Road and practically surrounded by malls. *$$*

The swanky Oriental beckons

DUXTON
83 Duxton Road
Tel: 227-7678
A boutique hotel (49 rooms) with a 5-star feel and facilities. Located in Tanjong Pagar, a post-war conservation area with lots of speciality shops, pubs and resturants. *$$*

FOUR SEASONS
190 Orchard Boulevard
Tel: 734-1110
Relatively small (254 rooms) compared to the other major chain hotels but elegant and exclusive. Size does not matter as guests come first. *$$$*

GARDEN
14 Balmoral Road
Tel: 235-3344
A quiet 3-star hotel in a residential area. Away from the hustle and bustle yet relatively close to the city. *$*

GOODWOOD PARK
22 Scotts Road
Tel: 737-7411
Grand looking, now a national landmark. Built in 1900 and has been a hotel since 1929. Still has lots of colonial-era charm. Excellent food and beverage facilities. A favourite of the Sultan of Brunei who even had his own suite there (until he bought his own hotel). *$$$*

HILTON INTERNATIONAL
581 Orchard Road
Tel: 737-2233
One of Singapore's oldest hotels on the Orchard strip but has kept itself up-to-date rather well. Has a swanky shopping arcade with everything from Cartier and Louis Vuitton to Davidoff Cigar boutiques. *$$$*

IMPERIAL
1 Jalan Rumbia
Tel: 737-1666
Located on a small hill overlooking River Valley Road (and the Chettiar temple in Tank Road). It's also well known for its superb North Indian restaurant. *$$*

Boutique-style Duxton hotel

LADYHILL
1 Lady Hill Road
Tel: 737-2111
Has seen better days but rates are reasonable. Cozy with its motel style lay-out, and just a five-minute walk away from Orchard Road. *$*

LE MERIDIEN SINGAPORE
100 Orchard Road
Tel: 733-8855
Located beside Singapore's Istana (the President's official residence), and literally on top of Kopi Tiam, a huge food centre that serves local food at very affordable prices. *$$$*

MANDARIN
333 Orchard Road
Tel: 737-4411
Favoured by many discerning business travellers with a deservedly good reputation for service. Even other hoteliers reputedly stay here when in transit. *$$$*

MARCO POLO
247 Tanglin Road
Tel: 474-7141
Great location near the embassy row and the Singapore Botanic Gardens. Across the road is Tanglin Shopping Mall and the Singapore Tourism Board office. *$$*

MARINA MANDARIN
6 Raffles Boulevard
Tel: 338-3388
Home to possibly Singapore's biggest garden atrium. The bar is a great place to end the day with a drink. *$$$*

MERITUS NEGARA
10 Claymore Road
Tel: 736-0248
Extensively renovated to international standards recently, it has probably the only Singapore restaurant specialising in duck dishes. *$$*

ORIENTAL
5 Raffles Avenue
Tel: 338-0066
The service is top notch (and so are the prices) but the atmosphere may be too formal for some. *$$$*

PAN PACIFIC
7 Raffles Boulevard
Tel: 336-8111
Sited at Marina Square with scenic views over the harbour and busy Singapore skyline. Well known too for its roof-top (37 floors up) Cantonese restaurant with stunning sunset and night views. *$$$*

PHOENIX
277 Orchard/Somerset Road
Tel: 737-8666
A city hotel that's right on Singapore's entertainment belt. Prime people-watching at the Pleasure Dome disco at its basement and at Peranakan Place opposite. *$$*

PLAZA PARKROYAL
7500A Beach Road
Tel: 298-0011
Sited near the traditional Malay and Indian commercial districts. Has an excellent health-fitness club with jaccuzi and Balinese-inspired swimming pool. *$$*

RAFFLES
1 Beach Road
Tel: 337-1886
The Grand Dame of historic Asian hotels was fabulously restored to its former glory in 1991. Some feel that its original charm was lost in the process though. Suites start from S$650. *$$$*

REGENT
1 Cuscaden Road
Tel: 733-8888

Upscale hotel for business travellers who enjoy exercising their expense accounts. Personalised room valet service. *$$$*

RITZ-CARLTON
7 Raffles Avenue
Tel: 337-8888
Top choice. Guest care and comfort are not just paid lip service here. Star attraction are its bathrooms with huge picture windows looking out into the harbour. *$$$*

ROYAL CROWNE PLAZA
25 Scotts Road
Tel: 737-7966
Brunei royalty recently bought this over and brought it up to speed as one of Singapore's top hotels. *$$$*

SHANGRI-LA
22 Orange Grove Road
Tel: 737-3644
Royalty and presidents think its Garden Wing is still the closest thing to hotel paradise on earth. Latour, its French restaurant is excellent and always booked. You might have better luck as a guest. *$$$*

SHERATON TOWERS
39 Scotts Road
Tel: 737-6888
Just a two-minute walk from Newton hawker centre, Sheraton tries very hard and generally succeeds in being one of Singapore's friendliest hotels. *$$$*

WESTIN STAMFORD & PLAZA
2 Stamford Road
Tel:338-8585
Both sit atop the huge Raffles Shopping Centre. Conveniently located next to the City Hall MRT station. *$$$*

Marina Mandarin: the atrium

HEALTH AND EMERGENCIES

Health

Singapore's water is treated and safe for drinking, and the clean, green image of the city is a fact. Strict control is exercised over eating places from hawker stalls to hotels, and unless you over-indulge in chillies there should be no problem. However, if you need treatment, there are about 16 government and private hospitals as well as umpteen number of clinics for any eventuality. Consultation fees start at about S$30 in a private practice. It is always a good idea to phone your embassy for a recommendation.

Emergencies

In an emergency dial 999 for the police, and 995 for the fire brigade or ambulance service.

HOURS AND HOLIDAYS

Business Hours

Business hours are from 9am to 5pm and banks are usually open from 10am until 3pm on weekdays, and from 9.30 to 11.30am on Saturdays.

There are three Singapore Post branches which are open everyday: Change Alley (at Hitachi Tower, Collyer Quay) and the Cluny Road branches operate from 8am to 9pm on weekdays and till 4.30pm on weekends and public holidays. The Changi Airport Terminal 2 Singapore Post branch stays open till 9.30pm daily, including public holidays, for basic postal services.

Other branch post offices open from 8.30am to 5pm on weekdays and from 8.30am to 1pm on Saturdays. Some branch offices have extended hours and are open till 8pm on one weekday night.

Shops open from about 10am to 8pm and many department stores are open until 9pm. Most shops are open on Sundays.

Public Holidays

New Year's Day: 1 January
Hari Raya Puasa: Date varies
Chinese New Year: January/February

Good Friday: March/April
Labour Day: 1 May
Vesak Day: May
National Day: 9 August
Hari Raya Haji: Date varies
Deepavali: October/November
Christmas Day: 25 December

COMMUNICATIONS AND NEWS

Telephone and Postal Services

To call abroad directly, first dial the international access code 001, followed by the country code: Australia (61); France (33); Germany (49); Italy (39); Japan (81); Netherlands (31); Spain (34); UK (44); US and Canada (1). If using a US credit phone card, dial the company's access number, followed by 01 and then the country code. Sprint, tel: 800-0877; AT&T, tel: 800-0011; MCI, tel: 800-0012.

Public telephones are easy to find and local calls cost 10 cents for every three minutes. Clearly marked phones can be used for world-wide calls. For convenience, buy S$2, S$5, S$10, S$20 or S$50 phone cards for both local and overseas calls.

Postal services are fast and efficient. An aerogramme to anywhere in the world costs 35 cents. Most hotels will handle mail for you or you may post letters and parcels yourself at any post office, where you may also send faxes.

Newspapers

The Straits Times and *The Business Times* are local English language dailies, carrying local and international news, with the tabloid *The New Paper* appearing in the afternoons. The *International Herald Tribune* is available on the day of publication. From Britain. The *International Express* is faxed from London and also printed here.

Radio

The Radio Corporation of Singapore's (RCS) English channels are One FM (90.5 MHz), Symphony 92 FM (92.4 MHz), News Radio 938 (93.8 MHz), Perfect 10 (98.7 MHz) and Class 95 FM (95 MHz). The BBC World Service is on 88.9 MHz.

Television

Television Corporation of Singapore's (TCS) Channel 5 broadcasts the daily news, dramas and sit-coms in English while Channel 8 has Mandarin programmes. Prime 12 screens Malay and Indian programmes. Premier 12 focuses on cultural programmes such as 'Pavarotti in Concert' as well as sports and documentaries. RTM 1 and 2, and TV3 can be received from Malaysia.

SPORTS

Singaporeans are a healthy lot – smoking is discouraged (or prohibited at all air-conditioned areas), although there is plenty of *yam seng-ing* (cheers! bottoms up!) of brandy at Chinese banquets. They like to keep fit, be it in the gym or jogging in the park, so sporty types should feel quite at home here.

Golf is extremely popular and there are 10 clubs with plenty of beautiful courses. Most public parks have jogging tracks and there are tennis, squash and badminton courts, but in this climate, you may prefer the swimming pool or more exhilarating watersports like windsurfing or waterskiing. Most hotels have pools and fitness centres and many have tennis and squash facilities too.

Golf

Green fees range from S$40 for a 9-hole course on weekdays to S$200 for a full round at a championship course on weekends. Most golf and country clubs are open to visitors on weekdays. You may be asked for your proficiency certificate from a recognised club. Club rental costs about S$15–20.

CHANGI GOLF CLUB
20 Netheravon Road
Tel: 545-5133
9 holes.

JURONG COUNTRY CLUB
9 Science Centre Road
Tel: 560-5655
18 holes.

KEPPEL CLUB
Bukit Chermin Road
Tel: 273-5522
18 holes.

RAFFLES COUNTRY CLUB
450 Jalan Ahmad Ibrahim
Tel: 861-7649
Two 18-hole courses.

SELETAR COUNTRY CLUB
101 Seletar Club Road
Tel: 481-4812
9 holes.

SEMBAWANG COUNTRY CLUB
75 Sembawang Road
Tel: 257-0642
18 holes.

SENTOSA GOLF CLUB
27 Bukit Manis Road
Sentosa Island
Tel: 275-0022
18-holes.

TANAH MERAH COUNTRY CLUB
Changi Coast Road
Tel: 542-3040.
Two 18-hole courses.

WARREN GOLF CLUB
Folkestone Road
Tel: 777-6533
18 holes.

Fitness fun for two

Windsurfing

EUROPA SAILING CLUB
1210 East Coast Parkway
Tel: 449-5118
Offers either a day crash course or a
two-day course for S$92.70. Laser
sailing lessons are available on a laser
single-handed boat at S$309 for either
four half-day or two full-day. A laser
boat may be hired for S$92.70 an hour
and a six-man dingy for S$100 for a
minimum of two hours.)

East coast windsurfing

Waterskiing

BERNATT BOATING & SKIING
53 Jalan Mempurong
Tel: 257-5859
Skiing here costs S$70 per hour
(weekdays); S$75 (weekends); includes
ski hire, boat, driver and petrol. This is
the easier location and more fun if you
make up a group.

COWABUNGA SKI CENTRE
10 Stadium Lane
Tel: 344-8813
S$80 per hour for an outboard, or S$120
for an inboard tournament ski boat.

Canoeing

Canoes may be rented at S$6 for a single-
seater and S$8 for a double-seater per
hour. There are two locations where
canoes are rented: East Coast Park, the
Lagoon Food Centre; and Sentosa
Lagoon, near the swimming lagoon.

Cycling

Bicycles may be hired at S$5 per hour,
or S$6 for a mountain bike at East Coast
Park's bike-hire stalls and on Sentosa
Island where there is a 5-km (3-mile)
track around the island.

Tennis

Booking a tennis court costs about S$6
per hour, more if you play in the evening
under the lights. You may reserve tennis
courts at the following places:

KALLANG TENNIS CENTRE
Stadium Road
Tel: 348-1291

SINGAPORE TENNIS CENTRE
East Coast Parkway
Tel: 442-5966

TANGLIN TENNIS CENTRE
Harding Road
Tel: 473-7236

Squash

Court bookings cost S$10 per hour.

EAST COAST RECREATION CENTRE
East Coast Parkway
Tel: 449-0541

KALLANG SQUASH CENTRE
Stadium Road
Tel: 440-6839

NATIONAL STADIUM
National Stadium
Tel: 348-1258

Bowling

The cost of each game is generally
about S$3.50.

JACKIE'S BOWL
542B East Coast Road
Tel: 241-6519

KALLANG BOWL
5 Stadium Walk
Tel: 345-0545

SUPER BOWL
Marina South
Tel: 221-1010

VICTOR'S SUPER BOWL
Marina Grove
Tel: 223-7998

Airlines

AIR FRANCE
#14-05 Orchard Towers
Tel: 737-6355

ALITALIA
435 Orchard Road
#20-01 Wisma Atria
Tel: 737-3166

AMERICAN AIRLINES
108 Middle Road
#04-01 Bright Chambers
Tel: 339-0001

BRITISH AIRWAYS
300 Orchard Road
#04-02 The Promenade
Tel: 839-7788

CATHAY PACIFIC AIRWAYS
10 Collyer Quay
#16-01 Ocean Building
Tel: 533-1333

LUFTHANSA AIRLINES
390 Orchard Road #05-01
Palais Renaissance Shopping Arcade
Tel: 737-0094

NORTHWEST AIRLINES
331 North Bridge Road
#08-06 Odeon Towers
Tel: 336-3371

SINGAPORE AIRLINES
6 Senton Way
#01-07 DBS Building
Tel: 1800-223-8888

SWISSAIR
435 Orchard Road
#18-01 Wisma Atria
Tel: 737-8133

USEFUL TELEPHONE NUMBERS

Fire, Ambulance	995
Police	999
Flight Information	1800-542-4422
Meteorological Office	542-7788
Postal Service	165

Telephone Directory Assistance	100
Public Phone Directory Assistance	161
Time Announcing Service	1711
Assistance in Calling (local calls)	100
Overseas Call Booking	104
Flight Information (Terminal 1)	1800-542-1234
Flight Information (Terminal 2)	1800-542-1837

FURTHER READING

Historical

Sinister Twilight by Noel Barber. Coronet. Fascinating account of the fall of Singapore.
Straits Affairs. The Malay World and Singapore. Compiled by JM Tate. John Nicholson Ltd. Glimpses of the Straits Settlements in the 19th century as seen through the Illustrated London News.

Historical Fiction

The Nan-mei-su Girls of Emerald Hill by Goh Sin Tub. Heinemann Asia. Enchanting story set in Emerald Hill.
Tanamera by Noel Barber. Coronet. A compelling love story against the backdrop of World War II.

Classics

Collected Short Stories by Somerset Maugham. Mandarin. Fascinating insight into life in the colonies.
The Malayan Trilogy by Anthony Burgess. Penguin. Not strictly Singaporean but a must for those interested in this part of the world.

Local Fiction

First Loves by Philip Jeyaratnam. Times Books International. About growing up in Singapore. An interesting insight by a prize-winning author.
Little Ironies, Stories of Singapore by Catherine Lim. Heinemann Asia. Ups and downs of Singapore life recounted with great perception.

Index

ACKNOWLEDGMENTS

Cover	Alain Evrard
Backcover	Ingo Jezierski
Photography	Ingo Jezierski *and*
23B	Alain Evrard/Apa Photo Agency
2/3, 65T, 66, 72B, 73B, 75B, 80, 102, 113, 114	Jack Hollingsworth
50	Larry Tackett
74	Manfred Gottschalk
6/7	MITA/Apa Photo Agency
89	Sol Elite Bintan
Handwriting	V Barl
Cover Design	Klaus Geisler
Maps	Berndtson & Berndtson

Bhutan★
Boston★
British Columbia★
Brittany★
Brussels★
Budapest &
  Surroundings★
Canton★
Chiang Mai★
Chicago★
Corsica★
Costa Blanca★
Costa Brava★
Costa del
Sol/Marbella★
Costa Rica★
Crete★
Denmark★
Fiji★
Florence★
Florida★
Florida Keys★
French Riviera★
Gran Canaria★
Hawaii★
Hong Kong★
Hungary
Ibiza★
Ireland★
Ireland's Southwest★
Israel★
Istanbul★
Jakarta★
Jamaica★
Kathmandu *Bikes &*
  Hikes★
Kenya★
Kuala Lumpur★
Lisbon★
Loire Valley★
London★
Macau
Madrid★
Malacca
Maldives
Mallorca★
Malta★
Mexico City★
Miami★
Milan★
Montreal★
Morocco★
Moscow
Munich★

Nepal★
New Delhi
New Orleans★
New York City★
New Zealand★
Northern California★
Oslo/Bergen★
Paris★
Penang★
Phuket★
Prague★
Provence★
Puerto Rico★
Quebec★
Rhodes★
Rome★
Sabah★
St Petersburg★
San Francisco★
Sardinia
Scotland★
Seville★
Seychelles★
Sicily★
Sikkim
Singapore★
Southeast England
Southern California★
Southern Spain★
Sri Lanka★
Sydney★
Tenerife★
Thailand★
Tibet★
Toronto★
Tunisia★
Turkish Coast★
Tuscany★
Venice★
Vienna★
Vietnam★
Yogyakarta
Yucatan Peninsula★

★ = *Insight Pocket
Guides
with Pull out Maps*

Insight Compact Guides

Algarve
Amsterdam
Bahamas
Bali
Bangkok

Barbados
Barcelona
Beijing
Belgium
Berlin
Brittany
Brussels
Budapest
Burgundy
Copenhagen
Costa Brava
Costa Rica
Crete
Cyprus
Czech Republic
Denmark
Dominican Republic
Dublin
Egypt
Finland
Florence
Gran Canaria
Greece
Holland
Hong Kong
Ireland
Israel
Italian Lakes
Italian Riviera
Jamaica
Jerusalem
Lisbon
Madeira
Mallorca
Malta
Milan
Moscow
Munich
Normandy
Norway
Paris
Poland
Portugal
Prague
Provence
Rhodes
Rome
St Petersburg
Salzburg
Singapore
Switzerland
Sydney
Tenerife
Thailand

Turkey
Turkish Coast
Tuscany
UK regional titles:
  Bath & Surroundings
  Cambridge & East
    Anglia
  Cornwall
  Cotswolds
  Devon & Exmoor
  Edinburgh
  Lake District
  London
  New Forest
  North York Moors
  Northumbria
  Oxford
  Peak District
  Scotland
  Scottish Highlands
  Shakespeare Country
  Snowdonia
  South Downs
  York
  Yorkshire Dales
USA regional titles:
  Boston
  Cape Cod
  Chicago
  Florida
  Florida Keys
  Hawaii: Maui
  Hawaii: Oahu
  Las Vegas
  Los Angeles
  Martha's Vineyard &
    Nantucket
  New York
  San Francisco
  Washington D.C.
Venice
Vienna
West of Ireland